Table Of Contents

Prologue.

Throughout my life, I have witnessed how technology and communication systems have transformed how we live and work. More importantly, during my career in UK law enforcement as a detective with the British Transport Police (BTP), I observed how criminals adapted to these advancements—utilising the same technology to communicate and, in some cases, commit crimes.

I experienced the evolution of digital forensics firsthand, from the early days when investigators examined suspects' computers, mobile phones, and other digital devices. Back then, data was measured in megabytes rather than terabytes, and floppy disks were truly floppy.

My first encounters with computers at work were in the DOS era. The office computer—a magical cream-coloured box—sat in the corner with its black screen and white text, constantly demanding input. I often questioned why we had to write everything by hand on paper, only to repeat the process on a keyboard. It felt like a waste of time, keeping me from my real job—catching criminals.

My interest in computers and technology truly began at home with the release of Windows 95. I purchased my first computer from our IT contractor, who was frequently called in to fix the office machine. Computers were expensive then, and I remember paying for mine over an extended period.

Curiosity got the better of me, and one day, I opened the computer to see what was inside. That was it—I was hooked. I discovered a hidden talent for diagnosing and repairing computer faults. With little formal training but a lot of perseverance, I began fixing computers for friends and family, something I still do today.

I also lived through the birth of the internet—the days of dial-up connections, AOL, Netscape, and the frustration of being disconnected whenever someone picked up the phone. Those who have only ever known broadband and Wi-Fi find it amusing now.

My supervisors noticed my aptitude for technology at work and recommended that I train as a computer forensics examiner. I was assigned to the London BTP High Tech Crime Unit (HTCU).

During my early days at the HTCU, I was mentored by experienced colleagues and sent on various training courses across the country. The work was demanding, often frustrating due to the sheer volume of cases, but always exciting and vital to investigations.

After my initial attachment, I returned to my role as a detective and later an intelligence officer in the East Midlands. However, I frequently returned to the HTCU to conduct digital investigations for my cases.

In 2002, I was assigned as the Intelligence Officer for the BTP investigation into the Potters Bar train crash, once again working in London. This was my initiation into major incident investigations, dealing with vast amounts of intelligence, communication data, and the Home Office Large Major Enquiry System (HOLMES)—an essential tool for managing complex investigations. It became clear that intelligence and, more importantly, evidence could be found across various technologies and the Internet.

Following the Potters Bar investigation, I was offered a permanent role within the HTCU in London, commuting daily from the East Midlands. They were long and demanding days. As colleagues retired, I eventually took on the role of unit supervisor and earned a Master's degree in computer forensics. However, as part of a national shift, the unit was later civilianised, and police officers were reassigned.

I returned to my role as an intelligence officer and started teaching staff how to use the Force Intelligence System. I discovered a passion for teaching, gained qualifications in training, and expanded my portfolio to include the College of Policing's mainstream cybercrime course.

At last, UK law enforcement began to fully recognise the importance of combining intelligence material and evidence gathered from various digital sources—computer forensics, mobile phones, the Internet, emails, and other communication systems.

Upon retirement from BTP, I established myself as an independent training contractor and online investigator, continuing to teach and share my knowledge. Along the way, I have met incredibly talented professionals, trained investigators from various law enforcement agencies, and stepped into the world of commercial investigations. I have gained new insights and contributed to numerous cases.

I am not a Python scripting expert, nor can I code, and I am certainly not a hacker. This book is based on my practical experiences in online investigation. I have long believed that UK investigators, in particular, lacked a comprehensive reference guide tailored to their needs. While excellent resources are available, such as those by Michael Bazzell, an expert in the USA, there is a need for a UK-focused guide.

This book is my attempt to fill that gap. It is designed to be a companion to my training courses and a practical guide for those taking their first steps into online investigations.

I wish you success in your investigations and hope that the material in this book proves helpful in your work.

Best regards,

Tony Bennett MSc.

Acknowledgements.

I want to thank the following people for their support, guidance, and friendship throughout my career and for helping to make this book a reality:

Bill Henry – for teaching me how to complete a perfect prosecution file.

John Sidebottom – for recognising my abilities with technology and encouraging me throughout my career.

Martin McKay – for leading the way in the digital forensic world.

Colin Fry – for being my mentor in digital forensics.

Jon Blake - for being my friend, helping me in the private sector and writing the forward to this book.

And most importantly, my wife, **Michelle**, for her patience and unwavering support.

Forward.

For 21st-century investigators, the Internet holds vast amounts of information that can be converted into evidence or intelligence and cannot be ignored. It's the duty of every investigator to follow all reasonable lines of enquiry, and the Internet clearly falls within those lines of enquiry in the vast majority of cases.

I first encountered the use of the Internet in an investigation in the early 1990s, when the online environment looked very different from today's Internet, with social media, databases, streaming, cloud storage, and apps for just about everything.

Even in those early days, information about individuals, their interests, associates, and businesses could be located using technical traces, utilising only publicly available or open-source information.

Investigators' skillsets have had to develop at a rapid pace with the times, and we are now faced with secure social media profiles, hidden online resources, fake news, and even the 'dark web'. However, none of these issues presents an insurmountable barrier if you know where and how to look.

Conducting Internet-based investigations involves legal, ethical, and physical risks. We must always remember to follow the law, conduct ourselves ethically, and, when appropriate, protect ourselves online. Our investigations should be conducted to a standard that allows the material we obtain to withstand scrutiny in courts or tribunals.

In this book, Tony addresses many of the issues I outline above and seeks to provide investigators with the skills and knowledge to conduct legal, safe, and accountable investigations based on many years of technical and investigative experience. There are many resources that should form part of your Internet investigation toolkit, and this book is most certainly one of them.

I have known Tony Bennett for over 30 years; he is a conscientious, forensic investigator with a great attention to detail. We worked in law enforcement together and in recent years have jointly designed Internet investigation training programmes and resources.

Jon Blake Cheshire, May 2025.

(Former Metropolitan Police Detective & National Training Coordinator at The UK College of Policing with responsibility for Internet Investigation and Intelligence).

Introduction to Online Investigation.

In today's digital landscape, investigators and intelligence operatives worldwide must effectively gather information from the World Wide Web. Mastering online intelligence-gathering techniques and having a centralised list of resources can make the difference between success and failure in various fields, including law enforcement, employee vetting, due diligence, fraud detection, brand protection, and loss prevention.

The rapid growth of technology, websites, social media, and online platforms has redefined communication. The internet has removed geographical barriers, while advancements in devices, computers, and mobile technology have accelerated global connectivity, bridging cultural and linguistic differences like never before.

What is OSINT?

There are various definitions of Open Source Intelligence (OSINT). The National Police Chiefs' Council (NPCC), the national coordination body for law enforcement in the United Kingdom, defines OSINT as:

"Publicly available information (i.e., any public member could lawfully obtain the information by request or observation). It includes books, newspapers, journals, TV and radio broadcasts, newswires, internet, WWW, newsgroups, mapping, imagery, photographs, commercial subscription databases, and grey literature (conference proceedings and institute reports)."
📖 National Police Chiefs' Council (NPCC), 2021
🔗 https://shorturl.at/vp1fv

UK law enforcement has expanded its approach to OSINT by incorporating multiple disciplines under the term i3. This concept categorises the different levels of online investigative activities carried out by law enforcement operatives. It integrates roles such as strategic analysts, financial investigators, intelligence operatives, and computer forensic specialists.

The increased reliance on technology and the internet has significantly enhanced access to and the value of open-source intelligence, enabling investigators to collect and analyse information more quickly and cost-effectively. However, investigators are now faced with overwhelming data that must be filtered and transformed into actionable intelligence.

Despite its proven effectiveness, some organisations underestimate the value of OSINT. Yet, it frequently provides critical context to intelligence or evidence from other sources. In many cases, OSINT has produced actionable intelligence or evidence, leading to strategic decision-making.

📖 Bazzell, 2023

🔗 https://inteltechniques.com/.

While OSINT is often considered one of the simplest intelligence-gathering methods, it comes with challenges. The sheer volume of available data can be both an advantage and a hindrance, making data filtration and analysis the most complex aspects of the process.

📖 Rid & Hecker, 2009.

For years, OSINT has been used by government agencies and military organisations to gather intelligence and evidence. The corporate sector also leverages OSINT to monitor products, assess competitors, and gain a strategic advantage in the market.

📖 Pendergast & Faltesek, 2018.

How is OSINT Implemented in UK Policing.

In UK policing, OSINT is part of i3 (Internet Intelligence and Investigations) which is a structured and increasingly vital discipline used across national, regional, and local forces to collect and analyse information from open and online sources in support of criminal investigations, safeguarding, and threat mitigation.

How i3 is Implemented in UK Policing:

1. Specialist i3 Units

Most police forces have dedicated i3 teams (sometimes called OSINT units or Digital Intelligence teams) responsible for:

- Gathering internet-based intelligence (social media, forums, websites)
- Monitoring threats, public disorder, or criminal planning
- Tracing online identities or networks (e.g. fraud, child exploitation, terrorism)
- Supporting major crime, covert operations, or safeguarding

These units often operate under Special Branch, Cyber Crime, or Digital Investigation teams.

2. Training via the College of Policing

The College of Policing offers formal qualifications and courses for officers and staff, including:

3. III Investigator Learning Programme

- Teaches how to gather and analyse internet-based data lawfully.
- Includes modules on:

o Internet infrastructure
o Advanced search techniques
o Social media analysis
o Evidence capture and preservation
o Operational planning and lawful authority

4. Legal Awareness Training

Officers are trained on:

- RIPA (2000) – Regulation of surveillance and data interception
- IPA (2016) – Investigatory Powers Act and use of targeted capabilities
- PACE (1984) – Powers around seizure and arrest

5. Tools and Platforms Used

i3 units use a mix of commercial, law enforcement, and open-source tools:

- Social Media Monitoring – EchoSec, Xapien, Social Links
- Image/Video OSINT – InVID, EXIF.tools, Suncalc, geolocation platforms
- Web and Domain Analysis – Whoisxml, DomainTools
- Dark Web Investigation – Specialised access platforms (under strict control)
- Data Preservation – Hunchly, WebPreserver, and evidential capture tools

6. Cases

Examples of how I3 is applied:

- Public disorder monitoring – e.g., identifying organisers of unlawful protests or tracking riot activity online.
- Online grooming cases – tracing accounts, chat logs, and media used to exploit children.
- Terrorism or radicalisation – monitoring propaganda channels and influence networks.
- Fraud and scams – identifying phishing operations or tracing scam pages.
- Murder investigations – linking suspects to digital trails (e.g., search history, social media presence).

7. Integration with Intelligence-Led Policing

i3 supports:

- Strategic assessments (e.g. threat landscapes)
- Operational briefings (real-time online activity)
- Safeguarding (vulnerable individuals online)

It forms a key part of the National Intelligence Model (NIM) and is regularly used in collaboration with:

- Regional Organised Crime Units (ROCUS)
- National Crime Agency (NCA) • Counter Terrorism Policing

How do we commonly obtain OSINT?

Open Source Intelligence (OSINT) can be gathered from a wide range of publicly accessible sources. Below are some of the most commonly used categories and tools:

1. Search Engines
Search engines like Google and Bing are often the starting point for OSINT gathering. The way a query is constructed can significantly influence the quality of results. Advanced search techniques, such as Boolean operators and custom filters, can help refine search outcomes.
Google Advanced Search: 🔗 https://www.google.com/advanced_search
Bing Search Operators: 🔗 https://www.bing.com/search?q=search+operators

2. News Websites
Traditional and digital media outlets provide timely coverage of global events. News articles can track developments, timelines, and contextual insights.
BBC News: 🔗 https://www.bbc.co.uk/news
Reuters: 🔗 https://www.reuters.com

3. Business Information
Corporate websites and registries offer information such as executive names, company addresses, and ownership details. Aggregators like OpenCorporates consolidate data from multiple global registries.
OpenCorporates: 🔗 https://opencorporates.com

4. Content Sharing Platforms
Sites like YouTube and Flickr host user-generated videos and images, which can be valuable for identifying people, places, and events.
YouTube: 🔗 https://www.youtube.com
Flickr: 🔗 https://www.flickr.com

5. Academic Sources
Scholarly databases provide research papers and articles that support in-depth analysis of specific topics.
Google Scholar: 🔗 https://scholar.google.com
JSTOR: 🔗 https://www.jstor.org

6. Blogs and Archived Content
Blogs offer personal and professional perspectives that may contain useful insights. Archived versions of websites and blogs, especially deleted or edited pages, can be retrieved using tools like the Wayback Machine.
Wayback Machine: 🔗 https://web.archive.org

7. Government Websites
Official government portals are a vital source of public records, policy documents, legal filings, and regulatory announcements.
UK Government: 🔗 https://www.gov.uk

8. Social Media
Platforms like Twitter and Facebook contain vast amounts of real-time and historical content. Social media analytics tools assist in filtering and analysing user activity.
Social Searcher: 🔗 https://www.social-searcher.com

9. Deep Web

The deep web comprises databases and resources that are not indexed by standard search engines. These often require direct access or internal search tools.

Ahmia (Deep Web Search Engine): 🔗 https://ahmia.fi

10. Dark Web

The dark web is a part of the internet accessible only through tools like the TOR browser. While associated with anonymity and sometimes illicit activity, it is also used by whistleblowers, journalists, and researchers.

TOR Project: 🔗 https://www.torproject.org

📖 JSTOR study on the Dark Web: 🔗 https://www.jstor.org/stable/26297596

✅TIP: By understanding and effectively using these OSINT resources, investigators can uncover actionable intelligence, trace digital footprints, and build comprehensive intelligence pictures from publicly available data.

Establishing a Digital Footprint.

A digital footprint is the trail of data you leave behind when you use the internet or digital devices. It includes all the information that is collected, recorded, or shared about your online activity — both intentionally and unintentionally.

Types of Digital Footprints:

1. Active Digital Footprint

- Data you deliberately share:
- Social media posts
- Emails you send
- Online forms you fill in
- Comments on websites

2. Passive Digital Footprint

- Data collected without your direct input:
- IP addresses
- Location data
- Browsing history
- Tracking cookies

Examples of a Digital Footprint:
• Your Facebook profile and posts
• Photos uploaded to Instagram
• Items you've searched on Google
• GPS location logs from your phone
• Metadata in documents or images
• Shopping history from online stores

Why It Matters to Investigations:
• OSINT (Open Source Intelligence) relies heavily on digital footprints to uncover identities, patterns, and networks.
• Employers, investigators, or malicious actors can use digital traces to profile, track, or verify individuals.
• Understanding digital footprints helps in privacy protection, cybersecurity, and online investigations.

Digital Shadow.

A digital shadow is the part of your digital footprint that is created about you by others, without your direct control or input. It includes any data, images, or mentions that other people, companies, or systems post, collect, or store about you.

Key Differences:

Digital Footprint	*Digital Shadow*
Created by you (e.g. posts, comments, profiles)	Created about you by others
You have some control over it	You often have little or no control
Example: a tweet you post	Example: a photo someone tags you in

Examples of a Digital Shadow:

- CCTV footage of you walking through a city
- Location data collected by mobile apps
- Online reviews mentioning your name
- Someone tagging you in a social media photo
- Data bought or shared between companies (e.g. marketing lists)

Why Digital Shadow Matters in Investigations:

- It reveals involuntary or hidden traces of a person's actions or presence.
- Investigators use it to build profiles, timelines, and associations.
- It's often overlooked by the subject, making it useful for covert analysis.

Before Starting Your Research: Foundations of OSINT Investigations.

It is crucial to establish a strong framework before gathering open-source intelligence (OSINT). This helps maintain ethical and legal compliance, ensures efficient resource use, and reduces operational risk. Below is a step-by-step guide with contextual examples and references:

1. Briefing: Clearly define your research objectives:

• What are you investigating?

• What specific questions are you trying to answer?

✅ TIP: A clear collection plan is a core principle in intelligence gathering

📖 Ratcliffe, 2009, Intelligence-Led Policing.

2. Parameters: Understand what is already known internally:

• Check organisational databases, past reports, and prior investigations.

• Avoid duplicating effort or missing existing intelligence.

✅ TIP: Use tools like Excel or Maltego to visualise known data points.

3. Expectations: Define which platforms and sources to target:

• News sites, social media, business registries, forums, academic databases, etc.

• Ensure this aligns with your objective (e.g. corporate profiling vs. individual vetting).

4. Authorisations: Ensure proper authorisation:

• Especially relevant in public sector, law enforcement, and financial compliance settings.

• For example, surveillance under RIPA in the UK requires authorisation Investigatory Powers Act 2016

🔗 https://www.legislation.gov.uk/ukpga/2016/25/contents.

📖 NPCC (2021) OSINT guidance for law enforcement stresses legal boundaries.

5. Policies: Review relevant policies:

• Your organisation's data protection and ethics policies.

• Legal frameworks like GDPR (EU/UK) or the Computer Misuse Act (UK). ICO UK Guidance on Data Protection and Investigations.

🔗 https://ico.org.uk/for-organisations/uk-gdpr-guidance-and-resources/

6. Risk Assessment: Evaluate operational and reputational risks:

• Could your activity be detected? What are the consequences?

• Use anonymisation tools and VPNS if required.

7. Record Keeping: Document everything:

• URLS, screenshots, timestamps, access dates, and tools used.

• Enables audit trails, evidence validation, and legal admissibility.

✅ TIP: Use tools like Hunchly

🔗 https://www.hunch.ly for automated tracking.

8. Equipment Check: Ensure access to:

• VPNS, browser plugins, scraping tools, image metadata tools, and administrative rights.

• Optional: separate virtual machine or burner laptop for operational security.

• Ensure your equipment has correct time and date by comparison with an atomic clock. 🔗 https://time.is/

Open Source Investigation Checklist.

It is crucial to establish a strong framework before gathering open-source intelligence (OSINT). This helps maintain ethical and legal compliance, ensures efficient resource use, and reduces operational risk. Below is a step-by-step guide with contextual examples and references:

1. Define Investigation Objectives and Intelligence Base

- Clearly outline the 'points to prove' for your investigation.
- Collate and document any intelligence already held.
- Identify any gaps or hypotheses needing validation.

2. Develop a Communications and Profile Strategy

- Establish a target's communications footprint (email addresses, phone numbers, usernames, aliases).
- Define clear parameters and scope to avoid mission drift.
- Be mindful of legal and ethical boundaries in your jurisdiction.

3. Select Appropriate Tools and Equipment

- Choose devices with suitable levels of security and anonymity.
- Install essential software (VPNS, browser privacy extensions, OSINT capture tools).
- Prepare dedicated investigation accounts (e.g., clean email addresses, social media profiles).

4. Plan Folder Structure and Naming Conventions

• Create a logical file/folder hierarchy for ease of reference.
• Adopt a consistent naming scheme for documents, images, captures, and notes.
• Maintain a separate log or metadata file to track sources and actions taken.

5. Conduct Comprehensive Searches Using Variant Configurations

• Search using full names, nicknames, initials, username handles, and email variations.
• Adjust for regional dialling codes and phone number formats.
• Search with potential misspellings, character substitutions, and casing variations.

6. Secure Evidence Immediately

• Use reliable capture tools to archive web pages, images, videos, and metadata.
• Save HTML files, PDFS, and screenshots in structured evidence folders.
• Document date/time and method of capture for evidential integrity.

7. Utilise Full-Screen Recording Software

• Record investigative sessions to preserve full context.
• Create timestamped records to support any evidentiary chain of custody.

8. Apply Advanced Search Techniques

• Use Boolean operators (AND, OR, NOT) to refine queries.
• Explore regional-specific search engines and country-code domains.
• Conduct image-based, reverse, and geolocation searches where appropriate.

9. Leverage Publicly Available Databases

• Search electoral registers, telephone directories, and company databases.
• Explore mapping platforms, genealogy records, and court listings.
• Combine datasets to build profiles and cross-reference leads.

10. Investigate Social Media and Online Communities

• Search platforms like Facebook, Twitter, Instagram, LinkedIn, and TikTok.
• Use known emails, usernames, and phone numbers to identify profiles.
• Monitor public posts, groups, and comment threads for associations.

11. Examine Online Marketplaces, Forums, and Repositories

• Investigate sales platforms (eBay, Gumtree, Facebook Marketplace).
• Review specialist forums and repositories related to your target area.
• Look for advertisements, buyer/seller accounts, or community involvement.

12. Identify and Investigate Secondary Targets

• Research associates, relatives, ex-partners, children (Digital Shadow technique).
• Build secondary profiles to uncover hidden or indirect information.

13. Search for Peripheral and Contextual Information

• Investigate vehicle ownership, previous addresses, and employment history.
• Search media archives for news reports involving the subject.
• Collate any available information on patterns or historical offences.

14. Conduct Visual Media Investigations
• Use reverse image search tools (Google Images, TinEye, Yandex).
• Explore video hosting sites (YouTube, Vimeo, TikTok).
• Analyse public photo albums, profile pictures, and geotagged media.

15. Trace IP Addresses and Domain Ownership
• Perform WHOIS lookups on domains for historical registrant details.
• Investigate hosting providers, server locations, and DNS records.
• Use IP geolocation services for approximate tracing.

16. Utilise Translation and Multilingual Search Tools
• Translate keywords and phrases into relevant foreign languages.
• Conduct native-language searches for broader data discovery.

17. Analyse Digital Images for Metadata and Context
• Reverse image search for the same photos online.
• Examine EXIF data for timestamps, device models, and GPS coordinates.
• Study backgrounds, environmental clues, and other artefacts in photos.
• Strip and preserve metadata separately for evidential purposes.

18. Trace and Analyse Email Headers
• Extract routing information and originating IP from email headers.
• Identify sending devices, mail servers, and network paths.
• Correlate header data with other sources to build investigative timelines.

✅TIP: When conducting open-source investigations, always ensure compliance with local laws, regulations, and ethical standards. Document all investigative actions thoroughly to preserve the admissibility of gathered evidence.

Policies for Online Investigators.

A standard Acceptable Use Policy (AUP) is not sufficient for online investigators because it is typically designed for general users, not professionals conducting investigative work. Here's why a specialised investigation policy is necessary:

1. AUPs Limit: What Investigators Actually Need to Do

A standard AUP often forbids activities like:

- Creating fake profiles
- Accessing the Dark Web
- Downloading investigative tools
- Using VPNs or anonymisation services

However, these actions may be lawful and necessary for investigators conducting undercover, OSINT, or threat assessment work.

2. Investigators Need Exceptions to the Rules

AUPs are built on the assumption of minimising risk, but investigators often need to engage with risk intentionally — for example, entering hostile forums or examining malware.

A tailored investigation policy provides authorised exceptions, backed by risk assessments and approvals.

3. Evidence Handling and Chain of Custody Aren't Covered

AUPs rarely address how to capture, document, or store digital evidence, which is critical for investigations.

Investigators need clear procedures for:

- Screenshots and metadata collection
- Verifying sources
- Maintaining the chain of custody

This is beyond what AUP's are designed to cover.

4. Legal Safeguards Must Be Investigation-Specific

Investigators face unique legal challenges, like:

- Defamation risk when reporting on individuals
- Covert surveillance restrictions
- Use of personal data in open-source findings

A standard AUP does not guide users on legal boundaries specific to investigative work.

5. Professionalism and Accountability

AUPs are typically about preventing misconduct (e.g., no personal use of company email).

Investigators need a policy that promotes methodical, lawful, and defensible practices, not just rule avoidance but also best practice adherence.

In short, while an AUP is helpful for general staff, online investigators require a purpose-built investigation policy that provides clear boundaries, authorised exceptions, and investigative-specific guidance.

Online investigators need a business policy for online investigation because it establishes clear, ethical, and legal standards for conducting investigations. Here are the key reasons:

1. Legal Compliance

A formal policy ensures investigators operate within data protection laws (e.g., GDPR in the UK/EU), the Computer Misuse Act, and privacy legislation.
It reduces the risk of inadvertently breaching laws that could lead to legal action or penalties.

2. Ethical Boundaries

It defines acceptable investigation techniques and avoids unethical practices like impersonation, harassment, or deception (unless authorised and lawful).
This safeguards the reputation and integrity of the organisation or investigator.

3. Consistency and Accountability

A documented policy promotes standardised procedures, ensuring all investigators follow the same methods and checks.
It helps maintain quality control and allows for audit trails and review of decisions.

4. Risk Management

It reduces exposure to legal, reputational, and operational risks by setting protocols for handling sensitive or controversial cases.
It clarifies what tools are allowed, how data is stored, and how to avoid contamination or loss of digital evidence.

5. Client Assurance

Clients, whether internal or external, expect professional standards. A clear policy:

- Builds trust,
- Demonstrates due diligence, and
- Shows the investigator is qualified and compliant.

6. Internal Training and Development

Serves as a foundation for onboarding and training new investigators. Encourages continuous improvement through regular review and updating of procedures.

7. Supports Use in Court

If investigation findings are used in court or disciplinary hearings, having a policy helps prove that evidence was gathered lawfully, fairly, and consistently, improving admissibility and credibility.

Example Social Networking & Open Source Information Policy for Non-Governmental Business.

[Company Name]

Policy Title: Social Networking and Open Source Information Policy

Policy Owner: [Insert Department or Responsible Individual]

Version: 1.1

Approval Date: [Insert Approval Date]

Next Review Date: [Insert Review Date]

Contents

1. Introduction

All employees who access social networking sites (SNS) or websites containing personal information for operational or business purposes, such as research or intelligence gathering, must adhere to this policy. All activity must be conducted lawfully, ethically, and in accordance with this guidance.

2. Key Messages

- Conduct company business using company equipment only.
- If registration or identity masking is required to access information, STOP and seek guidance.
- Access only open-source materials.
- All online activities leave a traceable footprint.
- Internet use is monitored.
- Where interaction is required to gather information, authorisation and specific measures may be necessary.

3. Technology

Emerging technologies and platforms like YouTube, Facebook, and LinkedIn offer easy access to open-source information. Additionally, club websites, business directories, voluntary groups, and tools like Google Maps can provide extensive personal information.

It is essential that:

- Information is lawfully obtained and processed.
- Information is gathered for legitimate business purposes only.
- Employees comply with all relevant legal and ethical standards.

4. Equipment

- All online activity must be conducted using company-issued equipment.
- Employees must not use personal devices for company research or intelligence purposes.
- Appropriate processes and software must be in place to record and retain web content of evidential value for audit or review.

5. Definitions

5.1 Social Networking Site

As described by Ofcom:
"Sites that allow users to set up online profiles or homepages and develop an online social network, sharing personal information, photos, videos, and other content."

5.2 Friend

The term 'friend' refers to a "contact" in the online context, and not necessarily a personal acquaintance. Online friends may be people known only through internet interaction.

5.3 Open Source Information

Information is overtly and publicly accessible without registering or submitting personal details. If access requires such steps, consult an open-source trained manager before proceeding.

6. Training

The company will provide appropriate training to employees conducting open-source Internet research to ensure activities are safe, legal, and reliable.

7. Covert Investigation or Monitoring

• All internet activity leaves a footprint, making covert activity traceable.
• Covert intelligence gathering requires using "non-attributable", specially designated terminals.
• Employees must seek guidance from a trained manager before engaging in covert activity.
• All covert research must be conducted exclusively on company equipment.

8. Use of a False Persona

• The creation and use of false personas must be recorded centrally.
• A false persona may be established for legitimate business purposes.
• Use of another individual's photographs without consent is prohibited.
• Employees must not impersonate a known individual.
• False persona use must not bring adverse attention to the company.

9. Relevant Legislation and Reputational Risk

The Data Protection Act 2018 (UK) governs the collection, processing, and storage of personal data.
Human Rights Act 1998 – respect for private and family life, online and offline.
Malicious Communications Act 1988 – offences relating to sending offensive or false material electronically.
Communications Act 2003 – addresses online harassment and unlawful communications.
Computer Misuse Act 1990 – unauthorised access to computer material.

10. Reputational Risk:

Failure to follow this policy could result in significant damage to the company's reputation, including:
Breach of confidentiality or data protection regulations.
Civil lawsuits or regulatory investigations.
Loss of client or public trust.
Negative media coverage and brand harm.
Any breach must be reported immediately and may result in disciplinary proceedings, including dismissal.

Policy Ownership: [Insert department or individual responsible]

Approval Date: [Insert Approval date]

Next Review Date: [Insert review date]

End of Document

Example Social Network Policy for Law Enforcement Use/Government Departments.

[Organisation Name]

Policy Title: Social Network Policy for Law Enforcement Use

Policy Owner: [Insert Department Name]

Version: 1.0

Effective Date: [Insert Effective date]

Review Date: [Insert Review date]

Approved By: [Insert Commissioner Name/Board]

Contents

1. Purpose

This policy provides structured guidance for Government employees and Law Enforcement (LE) personnel conducting internet research and investigations, particularly on social networking platforms. It incorporates references to legal obligations, national guidelines, and best practices.

Social media is a valuable source of intelligence that can yield admissible evidence (College of Policing, 2021). This policy outlines a three-tier approach to ensure lawful and proportionate online activity.

Scope: This policy excludes overt social media engagement by public-facing departments like Communications Teams.

2. Legal Framework and Compliance

All activities under this policy must comply with:
Regulation of Investigatory Powers Act 2000 (RIPA)
Investigatory Powers Act 2016
Criminal Procedure and Investigations Act 1996 (CPIA)
Data Protection Act 2018 - Applicable case law (e.g., R v. McKeown [1997] 1 WLR 295)

Investigators must ensure that:
All online activity leaves a traceable footprint (e.g., IP address).
Covert activity does not inadvertently alert subjects.
Evidence is lawfully captured and admissible.

3. Internet Research & Investigations

Investigations should distinguish between public and non-public information. Publicly available data may be accessed without deception, but systematic or intrusive monitoring may trigger surveillance authorisation requirements under RIPA.

4. Three-Tier Internet Research & Investigations Model

4.1 Tier 1: Overt Internet Research

Accessing open profiles and public content.
Mark activities as LE-related where appropriate.
Surveillance authorisation may be required for systematic activity.

4.2 Tier 2: Covert Internet Research

Conducted by trained officers using standalone or covert systems.
This may include the use of pseudonyms or the joining of restricted groups.
Directed surveillance authorisation required under RIPA.

4.3 Tier 3: Online Undercover Engagement

Conducted by Accredited Covert Internet Investigators only.
Includes direct online engagement with subjects.
Requires 'Use and Conduct' authorisation under RIPA.

5. Account Takeovers

Even with consent, access to an individual's social media accounts constitutes covert activity. This requires:
Written consent from the account owner.
RIPA authorisation.
Engagement by Tier 2 or 3 accredited officers only. (Reference: College of Policing, 2023)

6. Hardware Usage

LE online investigations must be conducted using appropriate systems:
PNN-connected systems: For internal communications only.
Standalone internet-accessible machines: For general research.
Covert systems: For sensitive or undercover activities.

7. Evidence Capture and Handling

All evidential content must be captured using approved forensic tools (ACPO Guidelines, 2012) and securely stored.
Accepted methods: Screenshots, screen recordings, HTML downloads.
All activities must be recorded in investigative logs.
Seek guidance from the Internet Investigations Unit for tool selection.

8. Personal Use of Social Media

Personnel must maintain a clear separation between professional and personal internet usage.
No LE email accounts should be used to register on personal platforms.
Officers should avoid disclosing their LE affiliation or personal information online.
Assume all online activities are visible to hostile actors.

9. Disclosure Obligations

All internet research activities must:
Maintain a full audit trail, including dates, methods, and tools used.
Be stored and handled in accordance with the CPIA 1996 and data protection regulations.
Be ready for disclosure in any resulting legal proceedings.

10. References

College of Policing. (2021). Digital Policing – Open Source Investigation.
ACPO. (2012). Good Practice Guide for Digital Evidence.
National Crime Agency. (2020). Cybercrime and Digital Investigation Manual.
Criminal Procedure and Investigations Act 1996.
Regulation of Investigatory Powers Act 2000.
Investigatory Powers Act 2016.
R v. McKeown [1997] 1 WLR 295.

Policy Ownership: [Insert department or individual responsible]

Approval Date: [Insert Approval date]

Next Review Date: [Insert Review date]

Searching for Individuals.

Basic Information to Collect:

- First Name
- Last Name
- Age
- Company Name
- E-mail Addresses (Personal and Work)
- Phone Numbers (Personal and Work)
- Home and Work Addresses
- Social Media Profiles (Facebook, LinkedIn, Twitter, etc.)
- Personal Blogs/Website URLS
- Friends, Family, and Colleagues
- Miscellaneous Keywords that might be related to the individual

Once you have these basic pieces of information, you can begin conducting searches. Google and Bing should be your first points of reference, and once you find more details (e.g., their name), use that to uncover additional information.

Example Searches: If you know someone's name and location, you can refine your search like so:

- "John Smith York"
- "John Smith Buckingham Road York"
- "John Smith LinkedIn OR Facebook"
- "John Smith's email"
- "John Smith's work email"

These variations will help you cast a wider net and uncover more detailed information. When searching for people online, always be creative with your terms, as different variations may know people by their names or even pseudonyms.

Cross-reference using:
• Electoral rolls (e.g. 192.com)
• Social media (Twitter, Facebook, LinkedIn)
• Image search and reverse image lookup tools (e.g., TinEye, Google Lens)
📖 Bazzell, M. (2023). Open Source Intelligence Techniques recommends layering search queries and formats.

Example Subject Profile.

A subject profile is a structured summary of all known information about a person, group, or entity being investigated. It serves as a centralised reference that investigators use to assess, monitor, or take action.

SUBJECT PROFILE	

Date of Photo:	
Likeness:	Not known – 8 years old
Name:	Insert Name
Alias / Street Name:	
Age:	
Date and Place of Birth:	DD/MM/YYYY
Gender:	Male / Female
Ethnicity:	e.g. White: Albanian
Nationality:	
CRO:	
Passport Number:	
ID Card Number:	

Risk Assessment				
Known Risk				
i.e. Firearms, Corruption, PEP, Terrorism, Location, Vulnerable Persons				
Risk Assessment Completed Yes/No	Date		Person Conducting	
Structure of Investigation				
Organisational Risks				
i.e. Lack of Resources (Trained Staff, Finance, Equipment)				
Lack of Inter Agency/Jurisdictional Cooperation				
Corruption, Sources of Information				
Physical/Moral/Legal				
Constitutional Rights Considerations				
Communication Strategy				
Internal Briefing i.e. Frequency of Team Meetings, Record Keeping				
Legal i.e. Prosecutor Briefing & Decisions				
Media Strategy i.e. SPOC				
Details of Agency / Contact / Frequency of Briefing				
Limits on Information to be Provided				
International / Other Agencies				
Financial Provisions				
Budget I.e. Allocation, Sources of Funding				
Other Agency Funding				
Review Procedures				
Review & Evaluation I.e. Review Dates, Objectives Met				
Authorisation				

Example Investigator Log.

Name: [Investigator's Name]
Organisation: [Organisation Name]
Operation: [Organisation Name]
Subject: [Subjects Name]
Briefing and Tasking Date: [Insert Date]
Time: 07:00 hours - Received operational briefing from [Supervisor's Name] regarding Operation ******.
- Subject: ******.
- Notes from briefing recorded contemporaneously in Investigator's Notebook (Serial No. 546271).
- Tasked with conducting open-source research

Objectives:
- Identify any financial accounts held by the subject ***** to support financial enquiries.
- Identify any business interests associated with to the subject *****.
- Identify known associates linked to the subject *****.
- Locate and capture social media accounts useful for investigation purposes.
- Build a comprehensive digital profile of the subject.

Investigator Actions 08:09, 01/01/2025 - Checked system date and time against official atomic clock. Computer was 1 minute fast. Adjusted computer clock to match atomic time.
08:12, 01/01/2025 - Created an evidence folder labelled Operation Beanstalk on secured storage for all work and exhibits. 08:13, 01/01/2025 - Commenced open-source research.
08:20, 01/01/2025 - Captured a snapshot of the subject's LinkedIn front profile page (URL: [LinkedIn URL]). Saved as Exhibit OB01.

08:25, 01/01/2025 - Captured a snapshot of the subject’s LinkedIn employment history page (URL: [LinkedIn Employment URL]). Saved as Exhibit OB02.
08:30, 01/01/2025 - Captured a snapshot of the subject’s Facebook profile front page (URL: [Facebook Profile URL]). Saved as Exhibit OB03.
08:35, 01/01/2025 - Captured a photograph of the subject from the Facebook photos section (URL: [Facebook Photo URL]). Saved as Exhibit OB04.
08:40, 01/01/2025 - Continued systematic open-source research across additional platforms, including secondary business registries and social networking sites [Details if applicable].
Evidence Handling:
08:50, 01/01/2025 - Compiled a Master DVD containing all captured evidential material.
- Placed DVD into a tamper-proof evidence bag (Serial No. 5007650001).
- Signed and sealed evidence bag.
- Marked: "To be opened only under court instruction."

08:55, 01/01/2025 - Produced a Working Copy DVD for internal review and further evidential preparation.
- Verified integrity of Working Copy.

Log Conclusion 09:05, 01/01/2025 Concluded log entry.
Signed: [Investigator’s Signature] Name (Printed): [Investigator’s Name]

Example Exhibit Index.

This index details the evidential material captured during open-source research on *****.
Each exhibit has been appropriately secured and referenced.

Exhibit Number	Description	Source / URL	Date Captured
OB01	LinkedIn Front Profile Page	[LinkedIn URL]	01/01/2025
OB02	LinkedIn Employment History Page	[LinkedIn Employment URL]	01/01/2025
OB03	Facebook Profile Front Page	[Facebook Profile URL]	01/01/2025
OB04	Photograph from Facebook Photos Page	[Facebook Photo URL]	01/01/2025
OB05	Master DVD containing collected open-source exhibits	N/A	01/01/2025

Foreign Name Search Guide: Best Practices, Challenges & Case Studies.

Understand Naming Conventions

- Research cultural naming structures (e.g., surname placement, patronymics, dual surnames).
- Avoid assuming the last word is the surname.

Example:

Western: John Smith

Chinese: Zhang Wei (Zhang is the family name)

Account for Transliteration & Spelling Variations

- Identify possible English spellings of the name.
- Use wildcards (*) and OR operators in search queries.
- Search using phonetic or alternative spellings.

Example:

'Mohammad' OR 'Muhammed' OR 'Mohamed'

Use Regional Search Engines

- Try country-specific engines like Yandex (Russia), Baidu (China), or Naver (Korea).
- Use Google with country-specific domains (e.g., google.co.in).

Example:

Searching 'Иван Петров' in Yandex yields more local results than Google UK.

Search in Native Language

- Use transliteration tools or Google Translate to convert names.
- Search using both Latin and native scripts with quotation marks.

Example:

"张伟" AND site:cn

Explore Official and Social Sources

- Look at LinkedIn, Facebook, and Twitter with location filters.
- Check local databases, directories, and company registries.

Try Reverse Name Searches

- Use username search tools (e.g., Namechk).
- Reverse search images or emails if available.

Example:

Search LinkedIn for 'Ali Mansour' with 'Beirut' location filter.

Track All Variations

- Create a name map with spelling variations, aliases, and nicknames.
- Keep records for consistency across searches.

Example Table:

Name Variant	Region
Mohamed	Egypt
Muhammad	Pakistan

Be Culturally Sensitive

- Recognise cultural differences in names and titles.
- Be cautious of gender assumptions or misidentification.

Example:

'Kim' can be a male name in Korea, but typically female in the West.

Challenges of Searching in Foreign Languages.

Transliteration and Inconsistent Spellings

Names from Arabic, Cyrillic, or Chinese may be transliterated in multiple ways.

Example:

Muammar Gaddafi = Qaddafi, Kaddafi, Qadhafi

Language Barriers and Meaning Loss

Literal translations may misrepresent terms.

Example:

'Minister of Culture' may translate poorly or differently in local languages.

Different Alphabets and Scripts

Searching in Latin script alone may miss local content.

Example:

Searching '张伟' in Chinese returns more accurate results.

Search Engine Limitations

Search engines may bias results based on your language/location.

Tip: Use VPN and localised versions of search engines. Local Context and Cultural Nuance Names, words, and references can be highly contextual.

Example:

'Papa Doc' in Haiti refers to François Duvalier, who is hard to trace if unaware.

Content Availability & Censorship
Some governments censor content.
✅ TIP: Use the Wayback Machine to view censored pages.

Name Order and Formatting Differences
Names vary across cultures.
Example:
'Kim Min-Jun' is Min-Jun of the Kim family in Korea.

Case Studies

Case Study 1: Chinese Name Investigation The investigator searched for 'Wei Zhang' in Canada but got limited results. **Solution:** Switched to '张伟' and searched on Weibo and Chinese business directories.
Result: The complete profile was on Baidu and the corporate listing.

Case Study 2: Middle Eastern Alias Trace Name: Ahmad Al-Masri Challenge: Multiple spellings including 'Ahmet', 'Ahmed', 'El Masry'
Approach: Used wildcards in Google, OR operators, and reverse image search on the known photo.
Result: Found a match via Facebook using Arabic script: أحمد المصري

Case Study 3: Russian Business Lookup Name: Ivan Petrov (Иван Петров)
Challenge: Common name with many duplicates.
Solution: Searched in Yandex with city + company + tax ID.
Result: Identified the correct person via the business registry in Moscow.

Searching for Companies

The process is generally more straightforward when investigating a company, as many business details are public.

Key Information to Gather:
- Company Name
- Year of Establishment
- Directors/Executives
- Company Website
- Phone Number and Address
- Employee Information (LinkedIn, HR contacts, job listings)
- Social Media Presence (Facebook, Twitter, LinkedIn).
- Company registries:

OpenCorporates: 🔗 https://opencorporates.com
Companies House (UK): 🔗
https://www.gov.uk/government/organisations/companies-house
- Leaked financials and offshore connections:

Offshore Leaks Database: 🔗 https://offshoreleaks.icij.org
✅ TIP: Cross-check director names with LinkedIn or press releases for further intel.

Searching When You Have Some Data

Once you have some initial data, it's time to perform focused searches. Here's an example to illustrate this process:

Example Data:
• Name: John Doe
• Born: 15th March 1980
• Address: 123 Elm Street, London, UK
• Phone Number: +44 1234 567890
• Occupation: Software Developer

Example Search Queries:
• "John Doe Elm Street London"
• "John Doe, software developer"
• "John Doe LinkedIn"
• "John Doe phone number +44 1234 567890"
• "John Doe email"

✅ TIP: You can combine your information and search for additional sources, such as LinkedIn, Facebook, or professional forums.

An Investigation Decision Log.

An Investigation Decision Log is a formal, chronological record of key decisions made during the course of an investigation. It captures who made the decision, when it was made, why it was made, and what the expected outcome or rationale was.

Purpose:

1. Transparency and Accountability - It clearly shows what decisions were made, by whom, and why, making the investigation process open to review.

2. Legal and Evidential Integrity - Helps prove that actions taken during an investigation were reasonable, necessary, and proportionate, especially in legal or disciplinary proceedings.

3. Audit Trail - For Oversight Regulatory bodies, internal reviewers, or courts may ask how or why certain investigative routes were taken. The log provides a ready-made audit trail.

4. Decision Justification - Investigators often work under pressure. This log helps justify why one lead was pursued over another, based on the available evidence at the time.

5. Team Continuity - If investigators change or the case is handed over, the log ensures that new team members understand the rationale behind past decisions.

6. Risk Management - It shows that risks were assessed and managed consciously, which is especially important in sensitive or high-profile cases.

7. Professionalism and Best Practice - Using a log demonstrates adherence to investigative standards and protocols, which is particularly valued in regulated sectors like policing, law, and private investigation.

What It Typically Includes:

- Date & Time of Decision:
- Decision Maker (name, role, badge number if police)
- Details of the Decision (what was decided and why)
- Information Available at the Time (e.g., intelligence, witness statement)
- Alternatives Considered Risks & Justifications
- Action Taken Following the Decision

Advanced Search Techniques.

Effective online investigation requires more than just a basic Google search. These advanced techniques can help refine your search, uncover hidden data, and improve your results.

1. Search Query Variation Varying your search syntax can uncover different results:

- Use quotation marks for exact matches:

"John A. Smith" Manchester

"J.A. Smith" AND "consultant"

- Use Boolean operators:

AND, OR, NOT (e.g., "John Smith" AND "engineer" NOT "teacher")

- Use the site: operator to limit your search to specific domains:

"John Smith" site:linkedin.com

"court records" site: .gov.uk

2. Phone Number Formats

Phone numbers are often crucial pieces of data for tracking down further information. Here's how to structure your search queries to find a number online:
Example Number: 07468810993

Try searching using various formats like:

- "07468810993" OR "07468 810 993"
- "+447468810993" OR "+44 7468 810 993"

You can automate this search using Opsimathy's Phone Number Search Tool.
🔗https://www.opsimathy.co.uk/opsimathy-toolkit/

For non-UK numbers, use similar formats by applying the correct country code. For example, a Chinese number could be searched as:

• "+86 1051924000" OR "01051924000"

3. Meta-Search Engines

These tools query multiple search engines at once, offering a broader view and helping to overcome filter bubbles:

• DuckDuckGo 🔗 https://duckduckgo.com/
• Dogpile 🔗 https://www.dogpile.com/
• Qwant 🔗 https://www.qwant.com/

International Search Engines.

Different regions favour different engines—use them for country-specific results:

• Yandex (Russia) 🔗 https://yandex.com/
• Baidu (China) 🔗 http://www.baidu.com/
• Naver (South Korea) 🔗 https://www.naver.com/
• Yamli (Arabic) 🔗 https://www.yamli.com/
• Search Engine Colossus – a directory of regional search engines worldwide 🔗 https://www.searchenginecolossus.com/

Clustering & Computational Tools.

Organise and analyse search results more effectively:

Carrot2 clusters search results into topics or themes, helping spot patterns and eliminate irrelevant data.

🔗 https://search.carrot2.org/#/web

Combining these techniques and tools allows OSINT researchers to uncover more comprehensive, accurate, and targeted intelligence. Each tool expands your digital reach and helps mitigate search limitations like localisation, personalisation, or content obfuscation.

Dangers of the Internet Filter Bubble.

The filter bubble refers to how search engines and social media platforms personalise the information you see based on your previous activity, preferences, and perceived interests. While this can enhance user experience, it poses a significant risk to OSINT investigations by potentially filtering out important, contradictory, or diverse information.

While this can enhance user experience, it poses a significant risk to OSINT investigations by potentially filtering out important, contradictory, or diverse information.

This means investigators may unknowingly miss critical intelligence simply because algorithms deem it less relevant to their profile. Over time, this echo chamber effect can severely distort situational awareness and objectivity.

For further insight, watch Eli Pariser's TED Talk: The Filter Bubble: What the Internet is Hiding from You
🔗 https://www.ted.com/talks/eli_pariser_beware_online_filter_bubbles

✅ TIP: To mitigate filter bubble effects:
Use incognito mode or non-personalised search engines (e.g. DuckDuckGo, Startpage).
Vary your keywords and search language
Cross-check results on multiple platforms and browsers

By recognising and counteracting algorithmic bias, OSINT investigators can improve data accuracy and maintain investigative integrity. Coupled with diverse tools and strategic planning, this ensures ethical and practical intelligence gathering, whether tracking people, analysing businesses, or identifying digital patterns.

Starting Your Research: Pre-Investigation Checklist.

Aligning with your organisation's objectives, legal obligations, and operational protocols is essential before initiating any OSINT investigation. The following checklist ensures a structured, compliant, and practical approach to online research.

1. Briefing: Define the Objective. Begin with a clear and concise briefing on the purpose of your investigation. Define:
• What are you trying to uncover?
• What are the key questions you need to answer?
A focused objective keeps your research efficient and aligned with organisational goals.

2. Parameters: Assess What You Already Know. Establish a baseline of existing knowledge:

- Check internal systems, past reports, and case files.
- Define the timeframe for research and what constitutes a successful outcome.
- Plan for alternate paths if initial searches return no results.

3. Expectations: Identify Targeted Sources Outline which sources you expect to use, such as:

- Websites, news databases, government registries
- Social media platforms, forums, and video content
- Deep web or dark web resources (if authorised)

Knowing where to look allows for focused and efficient data collection.

4. Authorisations: Ensure Legal Clearance

Verify whether you need formal permission or authorisation to:

- Access subscription databases or secure platforms
- Use specialist tools (e.g. scraping utilities, proxies)

Particularly important in government, financial, and regulated environments.

5. Policies: Know the Rules

Ensure you are compliant with:

- Organisational policies (e.g. use of investigative personas or pseudonyms)
- Legal frameworks (e.g. GDPR, Computer Misuse Act, Data Protection Act)

Breaches could result in disciplinary or legal consequences.

6. Risk: Assess Exposure

Evaluate the risk of discovery or detection:

- Could your presence be noticed?
- Would discovery jeopardise you, your organisation, or the case?
- Consider using:

Anonymisation tools (VPNS, burner accounts)

Investigative personas (if permitted)

Create a risk mitigation strategy before starting.

7. Record: Document Everything

Maintain detailed, timestamped records:

- URLS, screenshots, videos, metadata, and Notes
- Use tools like Hunchly or manual logs

Data can disappear or be altered—record it as you find it.

8. Equipment: Prepare Your Tools

Ensure you have the proper setup:

- Unrestricted internet access and administrative rights
- Access to necessary OSINT tools and platforms
- VPNS, proxies, or dedicated research environments (VMS or secure browsers)

A well-prepared setup prevents workflow interruptions and ensures data security.

By taking these preparatory steps, OSINT practitioners improve their chances of success and uphold ethical standards and legal safeguards throughout the investigation process.

Searching for People: Building a Digital Profile.

Conducting a successful OSINT investigation into an individual requires a methodical approach. Begin by gathering all known details and use them to build and refine your search progressively.

Step 1: Collect Basic Information

Start with the core personal data points you already have. These form the foundation of your investigation:

- Full Name (first, middle, last)
- Approximate Age or Date of Birth
- Current or Previous Company Name
- Email Addresses (personal and professional)
- Phone Numbers (mobile, landline, work)
- Home and Work Addresses
- Social Media Profiles (LinkedIn, Facebook, Instagram, Twitter, TikTok, etc.)
- Personal Blogs or Website URLS
- Known Associates (friends, relatives, co-workers)
- Related Keywords or Pseudonyms (nicknames, usernames, handles)

Please make sure to keep your data organised in a spreadsheet or intelligence file to track findings and cross-references efficiently.

Step 2: Create and Refine Search Queries

With the information you have collected, you can now start searching using variations and combinations of those data points. Begin with general search engines such as Google and Bing to establish a baseline of visibility.

Example Search Queries If you know a person's name and approximate location, consider starting with:
• "John Smith" York
• "John Smith" "Buckingham Road" York
• "John Smith" site:linkedin.com OR site:facebook.com
• "John Smith" email
• "John Smith" "@companyname.com" (searches for work email domain)

Search ✅ TIPs:
• Use quotation marks to narrow down results to exact phrases.
• Use Boolean operators (AND, OR, NOT) to broaden or filter results.
• Add keywords such as "CV", "resume", "blog", or "contact" to find deeper content.
• Search usernames and pseudonyms across platforms: use tools like Namechk or WhatsMyName to check availability across multiple services.

Expand the Search
Once you start collecting more identifiers:
• Use reverse image search tools (e.g., Google Images, TinEye) to match profile pictures across platforms.
• Look up email addresses or phone numbers with tools like:
Have I Been Pwned (for breached emails): 🔗 https://haveibeenpwned.com
Phone Validator or Sync.me (for phone number lookups)
• Explore social connections using graphing tools like Maltego or SpiderFoot.

Be Creative and Ethical

People don't always use their full legal names or primary contact details online. Consider:

- Common nicknames or name variations (Jonathan vs Jon)
- Maiden names or name changes
- Typo-based usernames or alternative spellings
- Comments, tags, or interactions on others' profiles

Important: Always operate within the bounds of legal and ethical standards. Respect data protection laws (such as GDPR) and your organisation's guidelines regarding investigative conduct.

Searching for a Company: Corporate OSINT Essentials.

Investigating a company is often more straightforward than profiling an individual, as businesses are subject to regulatory disclosure requirements. A combination of open data registries, official websites, and social media presence can reveal a wealth of information.

Key Information to Collect

Start by gathering and verifying the following details:
• Company Name (including registered variations)
• Year of Establishment
• Directors / Key Executives (CEO, CFO, etc.)
• Company Website & Domains
• Phone Number(s) and Physical Address
• Employee Information
Staff names on LinkedIn
HR contacts or recruiter emails from job listings
• Social Media Presence
Corporate profiles on LinkedIn, Facebook, Twitter, Instagram, Glassdoor
• Miscellaneous
Industry affiliations, press releases, known clients, or suppliers

✅TIP: Cross-check data from multiple sources to verify accuracy and uncover inconsistencies (a red flag in fraud investigations).

Where to Search - Key OSINT Resources.

Use the following trusted tools and databases to gather official company data:

Company Registries & Corporate Databases

• OpenCorporates: The largest open database of companies worldwide, with registration, director, and status data.

🔗 https://opencorporates.com/

• Aleph – OCCRP: Investigative platform from the Organised Crime and Corruption Reporting Project, featuring leaks and global company linkages.

🔗 https://aleph.occrp.org/

• Offshore Leaks (ICIJ): Database of offshore entities and individuals connected to financial secrecy jurisdictions.

🔗 https://offshoreleaks.icij.org/

UK-Specific Tools

• Companies House: The UK's official corporate registry.

🔗 https://find-and-update.company-information.service.gov.uk/

Search for:

Incorporation documents

Director of history

Annual financial reports

Company status (active/dissolved)

Additional Sources

• WHOIS Lookup Tools (e.g., 🔗 https://who.is): Check domain registration details to identify registrants, admin contacts, and creation dates.

• Job Boards (e.g., Indeed, Glassdoor): Job postings can reveal expansion plans, technology use, and organisational structure clues.

Practical Search Examples

• "Acme Engineering Ltd" site:linkedin.com
• "Acme Engineering" CEO email
• "Acme Engineering" filetype: pdf (to locate public reports or presentations)
• "Acme Engineering" site:glassdoor.co.uk (for employee insights or complaints)

Red Flags to Watch For

• Frequent director changes or dissolved/reformed companies
• Missing or hidden WHOIS data
• Inconsistent business addresses or untraceable office locations
• Offshore entities with no physical presence or operations

✅TIP: Always log your findings, take screenshots, and Note the source and timestamp—corporate websites and online profiles can change rapidly.

Moving from Broad to Focused OSINT Searches.

Example Subject Profile (Initial Data Collected)

- Name: John Doe
- Date of Birth: 15th March 1980
- Address: 123 Elm Street, London, UK
- Phone Number: +44 1234 567890
- Occupation: Software Developer

Once you've collected initial data points on a subject, it's time to pivot from broad exploration to focused search strategies. This stage aims to connect data elements and uncover deeper layers of information using specific combinations and targeted queries.

Focused Search Queries

Use the collected data to create specific search queries across platforms. The following examples illustrate how to combine and structure this information:

Name + Address

- "John Doe", Elm Street, London — Helps identify property listings, social media check-ins, or online mentions

Name + Occupation

- "John Doe, "software developer" — Useful for uncovering CVS, blog posts, conference talks, or developer forums

Name + Social Media Platform
• "John Doe" site:linkedin.com
• "John Doe" site:facebook.com — Directs search to specific platforms where personal/professional profiles may exist
Name + Phone Number
• "John Doe" +44 1234 567890" — Can reveal listings, classifieds, or leaks
Name + Email
• "John Doe" email
• "John Doe" "@companydomain.com" — Use standard domain formats to locate work contact details or mentions in documents

✅ TIP: Use Boolean operators:
"John Doe" AND "developer"
"John Doe" NOT "musician"
• Use Google Advanced Search or filetype: filters (e.g., filetype: pdf) to find CVS or documents.
• Search known usernames or aliases across platforms manually or using namecheck tools.
• Check developer or tech forums (e.g., Stack Overflow, GitHub) for occupation-specific footprints.

✅TIP: By tailoring your search queries to the subject's known attributes, you significantly improve your chances of uncovering relevant, actionable intelligence.

Searching for Phone Numbers: Formats and Tools.

Phone numbers are valuable intelligence leads. They can connect individuals to online profiles, classified ads, leaked databases, business directories, and communication apps. However, to maximise results, searching across multiple formats and regional variations is essential.

Example Number: 07468810993 (UK Mobile)

To improve search success, try the following common variations:
- "07468810993"
- "07468 810 993"
- "+447468810993"
- "+44 7468 810 993"

✅ TIP: Quotation marks ensure exact matches using search engines like Google or Bing.

Searching International Numbers

For non-UK numbers, adapt your formatting to the relevant international standards. Example (China): 01051924000

Try:
• "01051924000"
• "+86 1051924000"
• "+86 10 5192 4000"

✅ TIP: Use local number formatting conventions, especially when searching region-specific search engines like Baidu or Yandex.

Recommended Tools.

Opsimathy's Phone Number Search Tool
• A browser-based tool that automates phone number searches across multiple search engines and formats.
🔗 https://www.opsimathy.co.uk/opsimathy-toolkit/

Other Useful Resources:
• Sync.me or TrueCaller – This is used to identify caller names linked to mobile numbers.
• Phone Validator tools – To check if a number is active or associated with Voip.
• Have I Been Pwned – To see if a number has appeared in a data breach.

Caution: Always ensure your phone number searches comply with local privacy laws and your organisation's policy. Never attempt to access private data through intrusive or unethical means.

Google & Bing: Advanced Search Overview.

Google Search

• PageRank: Google uses PageRank and other algorithms to rank pages based on relevance and authority. Learn more about how it works in Google's Search Quality Evaluator Guidelines.

• Advanced Search: For a more refined search, Google's Advanced Search page allows users to specify criteria like language, region, and file types.

• Google Operators: Using operators like filetype:, site:, and intitle:, users can narrow down their searches significantly. The full list of operators can be found in various Google Search support documents and external resources, like Google Search Operators.

site:, filetype:, intitle:, inurl:, and - (exclusion)

Example: "John Smith" filetype: pdf site: .gov.uk

• Google Hacking: Technique using advanced search operators to uncover hidden, sensitive, or misconfigured content.

📖 Google Hacking Database (GHDB), a collection of queries designed to uncover vulnerabilities.🔗 https://www.exploit-db.com/google-hacking-database

Bing Search

• Operators Supported: filetype:, define:, contains:, inbody:

• Unique Search Options: Bing also has exclusive operators like contains.

📄A comprehensive guide to Bing's operators can be found on Bing's Support Page. 🔗 https://rb.gy/ppemje and in body

• Often surfaces content missed or deprioritised by Google.

Understanding the Deep Web.

The deep web refers to web content not indexed by traditional search engines, such as private emails or databases, and typically requires specific credentials to access, including:

- Private forums and portals
- Dynamic database content
- Paywalled resources (journals, legal records)
- Email inboxes, cloud drives, or login-restricted data

Not to be confused with the dark web, which requires special tools (e.g., TOR) and access protocols.

The Invisible Web vs Surface Web.

The invisible or hidden web refers to web content that search engines cannot access, while the surface web is readily accessible. Please read about it on The Invisible Web, a report by the Pew Research Centre.

https://www.pewresearch.org/data-labs/2024/05/17/when-online-content-disappears/

Quick Search TIPs.

- Use Ctrl+f (Windows) or Cmd+f (Mac) to search specific words on a page.
- Use Google Translate to interpret foreign content or entire websites.
- Use time filters in search tools to find the most current or relevant results.
- Always verify the credibility of information using authoritative, cross-referenced sources.

By using a diverse array of search engines, avoiding algorithmic bias, and leveraging advanced tools, OSINT practitioners can dramatically improve their investigations' reach, relevance, and reliability.

Web Browsers for OSINT: Tools, Risks & Recommendations.

Web browsers are essential tools for online investigation, but not all browsers are equal regarding privacy, compatibility, or security. The browser choice can directly impact your research quality, efficiency, and safety.

History of Web Browsers.

Sir Tim Berners-Lee invented the first web browser in 1990 while working for the European Organisation for Nuclear Research (CERN).
A modern web browser renders a website correctly according to web standards without using hacks or workarounds. Browsers such as Firefox, Chrome, Safari, Opera, and Internet Explorer are technically considered modern web browsers.
Key historical milestones include:

- 1992 – NCSA Mosaic: The first popular graphical web browser.
- 1994 – Netscape Navigator: Dominated the market in the 1990s.

🔗 https://www.w3.org/History.html

Internet Explorer is now obsolete and poses significant security risks. In 2019, Microsoft confirmed that IE is only a “compatibility solution,” not a secure, standards-compliant browser.
📖 Microsoft Blog – “The Perils of Using Internet Explorer as Your Default Browser” (2019) 🔗 https://rb.gy/hg6net

Browser Overview & Recommendations.

Mozilla Firefox

• Open-source, highly customisable.

• OSINT is favoured due to its add-on support and privacy options.

• Compatible with extensions for screen capture, user-agent switching, and more.

Download Firefox: https://www.mozilla.org/en-GB/firefox/new/

Google Chrome

• Fast and widely supported.

• Excellent for language translation of foreign websites.

• Extensive library of extensions via Chrome Web Store.

Download Chrome: https://www.google.co.uk/chrome/

Secure & Privacy-Focused Browsers

These browsers are ideal for investigations requiring enhanced privacy or anonymity:

• Iridium Browser – Chromium-based with firm privacy defaults.
🔗 https://iridiumbrowser.de/
• GNU IceCat – A privacy-hardened version of Firefox.
🔗 https://www.gnu.org/software/gnuzilla/
• Tor Browser – Routes traffic over the Tor network for anonymity. Crucial for accessing .onion sites on the dark web.
🔗 https://www.torproject.org/
• Brave Browser – Blocks trackers by default; built-in ad-blocker.
🔗 https://brave.com/
• Pale Moon – Lightweight Firefox fork with classic extension support.
🔗 https://www.palemoon.org/

Private Browsing Modes.

Private browsing helps reduce traceability on local devices:

• Chrome: Incognito Mode🔗 https://rb.gy/v37dbt
• Firefox: Private Browsing 🔗 https://www.mozilla.org/en-US/firefox/privacy/

✍ Note: Private browsing does not make you anonymous. ISPS, employers, and websites can still track activity. It also doesn’t prevent spyware or keyloggers from capturing your data.

Cleaning & Maintenance Tools.

OSINT Effective online investigations depend on more than just search engines and websites. The correct browser configuration, privacy tools, and maintenance practices can enhance security and research accuracy.

• CCleaner removes temporary files, browser caches, cookies, and saved form data, helping to maintain privacy and improve system performance.

Download CCleaner: 🔗 https://www.ccleaner.com/ccleaner/download

Autocomplete: Convenience vs. Privacy.

Modern browsers offer autocomplete features for:

• Forms
• Usernames
• Passwords

While convenient, these can pose privacy and security risks if sensitive data is auto-saved or exposed to malware.

Chrome Autofill Guide: 🔗 https://shorturl.at/BDy0z
Firefox Autofill Info: 🔗 https://shorturl.at/sa93u

✅ TIP: Disable autofill in settings or use encrypted password managers with two-factor authentication.

Raw & Legacy Browsers.

Specific browsers should be avoided for OSINT and investigative purposes:

• Internet Explorer is no longer supported; it is vulnerable to exploits and incompatible with modern websites.

• Safari – Limited plugin/extensibility support and inconsistent behaviour outside Apple ecosystems.

✅ TIP: Use Firefox or Chrome for maximum flexibility, plugin availability, and OSINT compatibility.

Add-ons & Extensions for Investigators.

Browser add-ons dramatically extend the capabilities of Firefox and Chrome for digital investigations.

Firefox Add-ons: 🔗 addons.mozilla.org

Chrome Extensions: 🔗 chrome.google.com/webstore

Popular OSINT-Focused Add-ons:

• IP and Geolocation Tools – e.g., IPinfo, Flagfox
• YouTube Downloaders – Save media evidence
• Screen/Video Capture Tools – Document web interactions
• User-Agent Switchers – Disguise your browser's fingerprint
• Metadata Extractors – Reveal hidden data in images or documents

✅ TIP: Always verify the legitimacy of extensions—malicious add-ons can compromise your system.

Bookmarking for Investigators

Organised bookmarks enhance workflow and research continuity.
• Create folders by case, tool type, or subject area
• Save trusted sources, OSINT tools, archived data, and links to documentation
Chrome Bookmarks Help: 🔗 https://shorturl.at/owu3P
Firefox Bookmarks Guide: 🔗 https://shorturl.at/bsZ6s

✅ TIP: Export your bookmarks for other devices or to back up your investigation environment.

✍ Note: Selecting and configuring the right browser is critical to your online investigation's efficiency, security, and discretion.

📖 Please see my website for my online bookmarks pages:
🔗 https://www.opsimathy.co.uk/useful-bookmarks/

Key Best Practices:
• Keep browsers updated
• Vet all installed extensions
• Use private/incognito mode when needed
• Align all practices with legal and organisational policies

✅ TIP: A secure, well-configured browser is your front line in protecting both your investigation and your digital footprint.

System & Browser Security: Essential Practices for OSINT Investigators.

Maintaining a secure operating environment is fundamental to conducting ethical, practical, and uncompromised OSINT investigations. Below are critical components to protect your data, preserve investigative integrity, and defend against digital threats.

Windows Updates

Keeping your operating system updated is essential:

• Automated security updates patch newly discovered vulnerabilities.

• Delaying updates increases the risk of malware infections, ransomware, and exploits.

• Ensure auto-updates are enabled or manually check for updates regularly.

Browser Updates

An outdated browser is a security risk and may cause:

• Incompatibility with modern websites

• Exposure to known vulnerabilities and exploits

• Limited access to newer tools and extensions

• Always keep Firefox or Chrome up to date to maintain performance and protection.

Antivirus & Malware Protection

Modern antivirus software provides multi-layered defence:

• Detects and quarantines viruses, trojans, worms, and ransomware

• Includes real-time monitoring, behavioural analysis, and sandboxing

• Essential for investigators handling potentially malicious downloads or suspicious files

• Use reputable antivirus solutions and run regular system scans.

Firewalls

Firewalls act as the first line of defence against unauthorised network access:

• Inbound protection: Blocks malicious attempts to access your system

• Outbound protection: Prevents spyware or compromised apps from exfiltrating data.

• Ensure your system's firewall is active, and consider using an advanced firewall for investigation-specific environments.

Cookies and Web Tracking

Cookies store data like login tokens, preferences, and tracking IDS:

• Some cookies enable legitimate site functionality

• Others can be used by advertisers—or malicious actors—for surveillance

• Regularly clear cookies or use privacy-focused add-ons that manage or block third-party tracking.

Passwords and Authentication

Strong password hygiene is essential for protecting both personal and professional accounts:

- Use long, complex passwords with mixed characters
- Avoid dictionary words and personal references
- Implement multi-factor authentication (MFA) wherever possible
- Use a reputable password manager to store and generate secure passwords
- Never reuse passwords across investigative platforms or personal accounts.

Computer Footprints in Investigations.

Computer Footprints in Investigations Maintaining data integrity and operational security is essential for OSINT investigators. Using a dedicated investigation machine—preferably isolated from other networks—reduces the risk of contamination, accidental leaks, or unauthorised access.

✍ Note: Limit access to the machine and use anonymisation tools and clean environments before and after every investigation session.

Recommended Tools for OSINT computers.

CCleaner

- Utility cleaning system junk files, browser caches, saved form data, and temporary files.
- Helps wipe traces of past activity and improves performance.

Official Site: 🔗 https://www.piriform.com/ccleaner

Malwarebytes

• Industry-standard anti-malware software.

• Detects and removes viruses, spyware, ransomware, and other threats.

Malwarebytes: 🔗 https://www.malwarebytes.com/

FastStone Capture

• Screenshot and screen recording tool with annotation capabilities.

• Useful for documenting findings or online interactions.

FastStone Capture: 🔗 https://www.faststone.org/FSCaptureDetail.htm

Hunchly

• Automatically saves and timestamps every webpage you visit.

• Organises evidence and maintains a full audit trail.

Hunchly: 🔗 https://www.hunch.ly/

Proxy Servers for Anonymity

HideMyAss (HMA): 🔗 https://www.hidemyass.com/

ProxySite: 🔗 https://www.proxysite.com/

VPN Services (Virtual Private Networks)

Expressvpn has strong encryption, global coverage, and no logs. 🔗 https://www.expressvpn.com/

Nordvpn – Advanced security features, kill switch, thousands of servers. 🔗 https://nordvpn.com/

Protonvpn – Privacy-first Swiss-based service. 🔗 https://protonvpn.com/

📖 Additional Reading on VPNS: Protonvpn Blog on VPN Legality – A blog post detailing the countries where VPNS are illegal.

🔗 https://protonvpn.com/blog/are-vpns-illegal/

TOR Network Tools

Tor Browser: 🔗 https://www.torproject.org/
Tails OS: 🔗 https://tails.net/
Whonix: 🔗 https://www.whonix.org/
📖 TOR Project Introduction: 🔗 https://www.torproject.org/about/history/

Standalone Linux Systems for Secure Browsing

Tails OS – Leaves no trace; routes traffic through TOR.
Whonix – Forces all internet traffic through TOR.
Kali Linux – Advanced penetration testing and anonymity features.
🔗 https://www.kali.org/

Virtual Machine Platforms

VirtualBox – Free VM software from Oracle. 🔗 https://www.virtualbox.org/
VMware Workstation – Professional-grade VM tool.
🔗 https://shorturl.at/iQ2md
📖 Lifehacker Guide to VirtualBox 🔗 https://lifehacker.com/the-beginners-guide-to-creating-virtual-machines-with-v-5204434

Anonymous Email Providers

ProtonMail – End-to-end encryption. 🔗 https://proton.me/mail
Tutanota - Secure email provider with end-to-end encryption.
🔗 https://tuta.com/
Guerrilla Mail – Disposable temporary email.
🔗 https://www.guerrillamail.com/
📖 ProtonMail Blog on Email Encryption
🔗 https://proton.me/blog/encrypted-email

Secure Messaging Apps

Signal – Encrypted messaging with no metadata logging. 🔗 https://signal.org/
Telegram – Secret chats for end-to-end encryption. 🔗 https://telegram.org/
WhatsApp – Encrypted by default (owned by Meta). 🔗 https://www.whatsapp.com/
📖 Signal Privacy Practices 🔗 https://shorturl.at/r5lqw

Metadata Removal Tools

ExifTool – Extracts and removes metadata from images and files.
🔗 https://exiftool.org/
📖 How to Remove Metadata from Photos
🔗 https://www.ionos.co.uk/digitalguide/websites/web-design/removing-exif-data/

Web-Based Investigation: Tools & Techniques for Investigators.

1. ICANN and Regional Internet Registries (RIRs)

ICANN: Coordinates domain names, IP addresses, and root servers to maintain global internet stability.
Visit ICANN: 🔗 https://www.icann.org/
RIRS: Allocate IP addresses and Autonomous System (AS) numbers by region: 🔗 https://www.nro.net/about/rirs/
AFRINIC (Africa)
ARIN (US, Canada)
APNIC (Asia-Pacific)
LACNIC (Latin America)
RIPE NCC (Europe, Middle East, Central Asia)

2. Country Code Domains & International Domain Names (IDNS)

IDNS: Domains using native-language scripts (e.g., Arabic, Cyrillic, Chinese).
Be aware of homograph attacks where lookalike characters deceive users.
Learn about IDNS – ICANN
🔗 https://www.icann.org/resources/pages/idn-2012-02-25-en

3. WHOIS Lookup

WHOIS: Retrieves domain ownership and contact info.
ICANN WHOIS
Whois Lookup (Whois.com)
GDPR Impact: Personal data may be redacted. In the UK, full access can be obtained through official routes like:
Single Point of Contact (SPOC)
Communication Data Requests under the Investigatory Powers Act 2016
GDPR and WHOIS – ICANN
🔗 https://blog.dnsimple.com/2019/04/gdpr-and-whois-privacy/

4. Hypertext and Hyperlinks

Websites use HTML to connect pages through hyperlinks.
Record complete URLS during investigations—they may expose hidden paths or directories.
HTML Basics – W3C 🔗 https://www.w3schools.com/html/html_basic.asp

5. URL Shorteners

Shorteners: Bitly and Tinyurl make long URLS easier to manage.
Expanders: Use to reveal original links for analysis:
Unshorten.it 🔗 https://unshorten.it/
Unshorten.me 🔗 https://unshorten.me/

6. HTTP vs HTTPS

HTTPS: Secures traffic with SSL/TLS encryption.
Use tools to examine SSL certificates:
SSL Labs 🔗 https://www.ssllabs.com/ssltest/
GlobalSign SSL Info 🔗 https://support.globalsign.com/ssl

7. Website Evaluation

Check a site's authority, accuracy, purpose, currency, and documentation.
Guide to Evaluating Websites – UC Berkeley 🔗
https://guides.lib.berkeley.edu/evaluating-resources

8. Tools for Website Technology

BuiltWith: Detects tech stacks, CDNS, mail servers, and can show currency types in use on the website.
Visit BuiltWith 🔗 https://builtwith.com/
HTTrack: Clone websites for offline analysis.
Download HTTrack 🔗 https://www.httrack.com/

9. Metatags and Robots.txt

Metatags: Metadata for search engines.
robots.txt: Instructs crawlers on what content to index or avoid.
robots.txt Standard 🔗 https://rb.gy/qwwn48

10. Website Cookies

Cookies track user activity—review for privacy compliance.
Cookie Checker 🔗 https://www.cookie-checker.com/

11. Website Archives

Retrieve historic or deleted content using:

Wayback Machine – Internet Archive

🔗 https://web.archive.org/

12. Website Monitoring

Monitor site changes with tools like:

Visualping 🔗 https://visualping.io/

WatchThatPage 🔗 http://www.watchthatpage.com/

13. Reverse DNS & WHOIS

Reverse WHOIS/DNS Lookups reveal related domains or hosts.

Viewdns 🔗 https://viewdns.info/

14. Hosting Information

Discover server hosts, DNS, and IPS:

WhoIsHostingThis 🔗 https://whoishostingthis.com/

Myip. Ms 🔗 https://myip.ms/

15. Copyright Breaches

Investigate reported IP or copyright complaints:

Lumen Database 🔗 https://lumendatabase.org/

These external references provide valuable tools and resources to support website investigations, whether for identifying ownership, verifying security, or checking for legal issues like copyright infringement.

Investigating Pictures: Tools & Techniques.

1. Enhancing Images

Let's Enhance is an AI-powered tool that sharpens images, removes JPEG artefacts, and upscales images up to 16x without quality loss. It is helpful in improving low-resolution or compressed photos during analysis.

🔗 https://letsenhance.io/signup

2. Comparing Images

Diffchecker – Image Diff Tool: Compare two images side by side and highlight differences. This method is ideal for verifying image alterations or detecting inconsistencies in photo evidence.

🔗 https://www.diffchecker.com/image-compare/

3. Reverse Image Search

Critical for tracing the origin or distribution of an image online. These tools rely on Content-Based Image Retrieval (CBIR) rather than metadata:

Google Reverse Image Search 🔗 https://www.google.com/imghp

TinEye 🔗 https://tineye.com/

Yandex Images 🔗 https://yandex.com/images/search?from=tabbar

These tools can help identify the source of an image, detect edits, or find duplicates.

4. Exif Metadata Analysis

Exchangeable Image File Format (Exif) data includes camera model, timestamp, and GPS location. Key tools include:

FotoForensics: Offers image forensics such as Error Level Analysis (ELA) and metadata extraction. 🔗 https://www.fotoforensics.com/

Pic2Map: Extracts GPS data from images and plots the location on a map. 🔗 https://www.pic2map.com/

GeoSetter: Windows-based tool to view, edit, and map Exif metadata in bulk. 🔗 https://geosetter.de/en/download-en/

5. Tracking Stolen Cameras

Stolen Camera Finder: Scans web photos for embedded camera serial numbers to track stolen DSLRS.

🔗 https://www.stolencamerafinder.com/

✍ Note: Most mobile phone cameras (e.g., iPhones) do not store serial numbers in Exif data.

6. Screenshots and Snipping Tools

Use built-in tools like Windows Snipping Tool or Snip & Sketch when direct downloads aren't possible.

Be aware that screenshots may degrade quality and strip metadata—use cautiously in evidential contexts.

7. Admissibility of Photos in Court

Digital photos must be relevant and authenticated as evidence.

UK Parliament Guide – Digital Images and Evidence in Court.

🔗 https://www.gov.uk/guidance/digital-presentations-in-court-guidance-for-professionals

Investigating YouTube & Online Videos.

1. YouTube Search Techniques

• Use filters: relevance, upload date, duration, features (e.g., subtitles, HD).

• Use search operators:

"exact phrase": for precise matches.

+keyword: to include specific terms.

intitle:keyword: search within video titles.

• Short-duration filters (e.g., under 4 minutes) help find mobile or dashcam footage.

Google Advanced Video Search

🔗 https://www.google.com/advanced_video_search

2. Downloading YouTube Videos

For offline analysis or preservation, use trusted sites:

🔗 ClipConverter https://www.clipconverter.cc/nl/3/

Always ensure compliance with copyright laws and fair use principles.

3. MW Geofind

This is an online tool designed for identifying YouTube videos that have been tagged with a specific geographical location.

🔗 https://mattw.io/youtube-geofind/location

4. Frame-by-Frame Video Viewing

Use these tools to examine content in slow motion or per frame:

🔗 http://www.watchframebyframe.com/

Analyser helps detect hidden details, faces, landmarks, or identifying features. 🔗 https://anilyzer.com/

5. Verification and Forensic Plugins

Invid Verification Plugin:

🔗 https://www.invid-project.eu/tools-and-services/invid-verification-plugin/

Breaks videos into keyframes.

Reverse image search for thumbnails.

Checks metadata.

Applies filters like Error Level Analysis.

Invid Chrome Plugin

6. Alternative Video Platforms

Don't limit your investigation to YouTube. Check:

Vimeo 🔗 https://vimeo.com/

Dailymotion 🔗 https://www.dailymotion.com/gb

7. Screen Recording Tools

If direct download isn't possible:

Screencast-O-Matic or OBS Studio for reliable recording.

🔗 https://screencast-o-matic.en.download.it/

Srecorder is a free video recorder download. 🔗 https://srecorder.com/

Windows built-in tools: Snip & Sketch or Game Bar.

✍ Note: Recorded videos may not retain metadata. Use cautiously in evidence contexts.

8. Approach to Video Investigation

• Focus on keywords linked to location, events, or known terms.

• Use multiple tools to triangulate source and authenticity.

• Extract thumbnails and run reverse searches to uncover altered or reposted content.

Investigating Emails: Tools & Techniques.

Emails contain far more than just sender details and message content. For investigators, email headers and metadata can reveal routing paths, source IPs, and signs of manipulation or fraud.

Why Investigate Emails?

Investigators analyse emails to:

- Detect phishing attempts or spoofed senders
- View routing paths and server relays
- Trace the origin or IP address of the sender
- Identify hidden clues (e.g., fake domains, modified metadata)

The Three Parts of an Email

1. Envelope - Hidden, server-level routing data used in mail delivery systems.
2. Header - Reveals sender, recipient, subject, IP addresses, and timestamps. Headers are key to identifying source information and potential forgeries.
3. Body - The message content. May include links, attachments, or malicious payloads.

How to View Email Headers

Headers must be extracted directly from the original email—not a forwarded copy. Here's how to access headers on major platforms:

• Gmail: Open the message → ⋮ menu → Show Original
• Outlook: Open email → ⋮ menu → View Source
• Yahoo Mail: Open message → ⋮ menu → View Raw Message

MXToolbox – Email Header Retrieval Guide
🔗 https://mxtoolbox.com/Public/Content/EmailHeaders/

Key Fields in Email Headers.

Headers are listed in reverse order (most recent at the top). Could you start reading from the bottom up? Key fields to inspect:

Return-Path - Bounce-back address; valid for verifying delivery.
Delivery Date - Timestamp when received by the recipient's server.
Date - When the sender's system sent the email.
Message-ID - Unique ID assigned by the sender's system. Helpful in tracing threads.
X-Mailer - Mail client used (e.g., Outlook, Apple Mail). From the claimed sender email (can be spoofed). To the Intended recipient.
Subject - Email subject line.

✅ TIP: IP addresses in the earliest Received: entries often show the originating server and can be geolocated.

IPTracker – Email Header Analysis Tool
🔗 https://www.iptrackeronline.com/email-header-analysis/

Investigation Profiles for Social Media Investigation.

Key Principles

Believability: The persona must appear authentic within its digital environment.
Purpose-driven: Tailor the persona to the goals of the investigation.
Security-conscious: Avoid using real photos or data that could trace back to you.

Core Components of a Social Media Investigation Profile
Name - Use tools like FakeNameGenerator to create a believable name. 🔗 https://www.fakenamegenerator.com/
Email - Use a new email for each persona (e.g., Gmail, Outlook, ProtonMail or Tutanota).
Phone Number - Use a pay-as-you-go SIM for account verification.
Profile Picture - Use AI-generated faces from:
This Person Does Not Exist 🔗 https://thispersondoesnotexist.com/
Gallery of AI Faces 🔗 https://generated.photos/faces
Or avatar tools. 🔗 https://avatarmaker.com/
Location - Match the persona's location to the target's region (use VPN/geotags accordingly).
Bio/Description - Include realistic details: school, hobbies, slang, or hashtags relevant to the region or target group.
Social Proof - Add friends, followers, posts, and interactions to build credibility.
Activity History - Slowly build post history to make the profile look lived-in (back-date posts if possible).

✅ TIP: Snip images and edit them if possible before posting
Caution: Never use real photos of people's faces - you are not impersonating someone!

✅ TIP: Currently it is advisable not to start making investigation profiles with any of the Meta group Social accounts which means Facebook, Instagram, WhatsApp, etc. and their associated features, including the new Meta AI chatbot - this is due to enhanced checks to prove you are not a false account.

Platform-Specific Setup TIPs:

Facebook
Use real-life patterns: family, education, work, and photos of hobbies.
Join local groups or follow similar interests.
Keep a consistent posting style (quotes, memes, check-ins).
Facebook Graph Search is no longer available.
Avoid mistakes if possible.
If security challenge occurs you are likely to lose your account and have to start again.

Twitter/X
A Twitter account can easily be made from a Google email login
Engage with trending topics and hashtags relevant to your target.
Follow accounts that reflect the persona's interests.
Tweet regularly but avoid overposting early on.
Many of the previous Twitter tools no longer work since Twitter became X.

LinkedIn
Use trac.jobs .pdf or similar tools for creating job titles and companies.
🔗 https://apps.trac.jobs/documents?vdoc=9222779
Build a simple resume and work history.
Connect with others in the industry, ideally other personas.

✅ TIP: Avoid logging in to LinkedIn if possible, as it is likely your target will be notified you have viewed their profile

✅ TIP: Use Google Advanced Search techniques for LinkedIn searching, i.e. site:linkedin.com

Instagram
Post hobby-related images (e.g., food, pets, landscapes).
Use region-specific hashtags.
Follow local influencers and engage with posts.

TikTok
Post hobby or trend-based videos (even stock or repurposed).
Engage with location- or interest-based hashtags.
Use trending audio clips to build algorithm trust.

Security & Operational Hygiene
Use a dedicated machine or virtual environment for persona activity.
Enable 2fa (Two-Factor Authentication) with a burner number or app.
Never log in from your real IP—always use a VPN or secure proxy.
Maintain a persona diary: track creation date, credentials, interactions, and any changes.

Legal & Ethical Reminders

Check local laws: Some jurisdictions prohibit false identity creation on specific platforms.

Always ensure your actions align with your agency’s policies and legal framework.

Avoid entrapment, harassment, or illegal surveillance.

Why use an investigation persona?

Using an investigation persona in OSINT or online investigations offers several significant advantages, especially for professional or sensitive research.
Here's why it's used:

- **Protect Your Identity** - Keeps your real identity, IP address, and digital footprint hidden from the subject of the investigation. Avoids alerting targets who may monitor who is viewing their content.
- **Appear Believable in Target Environments**
A persona can blend into specific online communities, forums, or social media groups, allowing access to information otherwise restricted to "insiders." Helps avoid suspicion during passive or active intelligence gathering.
- **Circumvent Algorithmic Restrictions**
Some platforms adjust what you see based on your profile or behaviour. A tailored persona can bypass filter bubbles and show what a typical user from a specific demographic would see.
- **Localised Research**
Investigation personas can be built with specific geographic, linguistic, or cultural traits, making them more effective for region-specific investigations (e.g., a persona for Manchester vs. one for Dubai).
- **Enable Controlled Engagement.**
- **A/B Testing and Verification.** Multiple personas can be used to cross-verify results, test responses to inquiries, or track changes in user behaviour when different personas are used.
- **Maintain Investigative Integrity**
Keeps your professional and investigative activities separate, supporting operational security and documentation clarity..

Key Points for Creating an Investigation Persona.

1. Tailoring the Persona:
When creating an investigation persona, the details should mirror those of the person under investigation. For instance, if investigating a young male graffiti artist who is using drugs and drinking, the persona should reflect these behaviours. The persona's interests, race, occupation, and social circles should align with the subject's life to ensure authenticity.

2. Social Proof:
This concept refers to adding interactions, such as posts, friends, and online activities, to make the persona appear genuine. Social media activity should be frequent, with ongoing discussions or engagements. This may involve connecting with other fabricated accounts or creating content that reflects the persona's lifestyle and interests.

3. Multiple Accounts:
Sometimes, investigators create several linked personas to support the primary persona, further legitimising the character. This can also help gather more diverse information, providing a well-rounded picture of the subject's behaviour and interactions.

4. Tools for Creating Personas:

Websites like FakeNameGenerator can help generate initial personal details like name, address, job, and more. After developing these details, investigators can adjust the persona to suit the case's specific requirements, such as adjusting hobbies, professions, and locations to fit the target's lifestyle.

https://www.fakenamegenerator.com

5. Platform-Specific Considerations:

Different social media platforms like Facebook, Twitter, and LinkedIn require different strategies.

Facebook: The persona should reflect a whole life with friends, photos, posts, and interests. A pay-as-you-go phone number is often used for phone verification.

Twitter: A custom username, engagement with relevant topics, and following accounts related to the persona's interests will help establish credibility.

LinkedIn: Professional details such as employment status, job title, and company affiliation are essential for creating a convincing professional persona.

6. Profile Pictures:

Real photos should not be used, as they could be traced. Instead, investigators often use avatars, silhouettes, or images from platforms like ThisPersonDoesNotexist.com, which generate realistic faces that do not belong to actual people. Alternatively, cartoon avatars or hobby-related photos can work. https://thispersondoesnotexist.com/

7. Regular Activity:

The investigation persona should post content regularly to maintain the illusion of a real person. This might include casual comments on current events, sharing pictures about their hobbies, or conversing with other profiles. Interacting with other personas can also help the persona appear more social.

8. Legal and Ethical Considerations:
It is crucial to consider the legality and ethics of using investigation personas, as creating fake accounts could violate social media platforms' terms of service and, in some jurisdictions, even be illegal. Always ensure the methods align with your organisation's policies and the laws of the country where the investigation is conducted.

Conclusion: Creating a believable investigation persona requires careful attention to detail, social interactions, and maintaining an online presence that mirrors the subject's real-life behaviours. These accounts are vital tools in OSINT investigations, but must be used cautiously and within legal and ethical boundaries.

Key Information to Gather from Social Media.

A picture of the subject, email addresses, birth details, family members (mother's maiden name), children, siblings, colleagues, and known locations (home, work, vacations).
Don't forget to search for connections (family, friends) to expand the scope.

Useful Social Media Search Tools.

WebMii: People and company search engine, offering profile pictures and online visibility scores. 🔗 https://webmii.com/
Social-Searcher: Monitors public social mentions. 🔗 https://www.social-searcher.com/
192.com: Paid service for family searches in the UK. Look for family near your target's home. 🔗 https://www.192.com/
Truecaller & WhoCallsMe: Mobile phone search websites.
Facebook Graph Search is no longer available for plain language searches.
These tools and resources should provide a strong foundation for conducting thorough social media research

Metadata Extraction from Documents.

Metadata from documents such as PDFs, DOCs, and images can reveal author names, creation/modification dates, software used, and GPS coordinates (in images).

Useful Tools:
- ExifTool: 🔗 https://exiftool.org
- FOCA (Windows only): 🔗 https://www.elevenpaths.com/labstools/foca/index.html
- ExtractMetadata: 🔗 https://www.extractmetadata.com
- Metadata2Go (browser-based): 🔗 https://www.metadata2go.com

QR Code & Barcode Investigation.

QR codes and barcodes may embed URLs, credentials, or access links. Investigators can decode and examine these codes using free online tools.
Useful Tools:
- ZXing Decoder: 🔗 https://zxing.org/w/decode.jspx
- Online Barcode Reader: 🔗 https://onlinebarcodereader.com
- QRStuff (generator and decoder): 🔗 https://www.qrstuff.com

Mobile App Emulation & Analysis.

Some platforms restrict access to app-only data. Mobile emulation or APK analysis allows deeper access to functionality and app behaviour.
Useful Tools:
- BlueStacks Emulator: 🔗 https://www.bluestacks.com
- APKTool: 🔗 https://ibotpeaches.github.io/Apktool/
- Objection (Runtime Mobile Exploration): 🔗 https://github.com/sensepost/objection

Facial Recognition & Reverse Image Search.

AI-based image matching tools help track a person across the internet using face search or image clustering.

Useful Tools:

- PimEyes: 🔗 https://pimeyes.com
- Betaface: 🔗 https://www.betaface.com/demo.html
- FaceCheck ID: 🔗 https://facecheck.id
- Yandex Image Search (accurate reverse search): 🔗 https://yandex.com/images/

Aircraft, Vessel & Vehicle Tracking.

Transportation tracking provides real-time or historical insights into movements, ownership, and locations.

Aircraft:

Flightradar24: 🔗 https://www.flightradar24.com

- ADS-B Exchange: 🔗 https://www.adsbexchange.com

Ships:

- MarineTraffic: 🔗 https://www.marinetraffic.com
- VesselFinder: 🔗 https://www.vesselfinder.com

Vehicles:

- VIN Decoder: 🔗 https://www.vindecoderz.com
- DVLA MOT Check (UK): 🔗 https://www.gov.uk/check-mot-history

Blockchain & Cryptocurrency Tracing.

Cryptocurrency transactions are publicly visible on blockchain explorers, allowing tracking of addresses and transfers.
Useful Tools:
- Blockchain Explorer: https://www.blockchain.com/explorer
- Etherscan (Ethereum): https://etherscan.io
- Chainalysis (Professional): https://www.chainalysis.com
- CipherTrace (Enterprise): https://ciphertrace.com

Leaked Credentials & Data Breach Monitoring.

Compromised data in breaches can reveal passwords, emails, or sensitive information linked to your target.
Useful Tools:
- Have I Been Pwned: https://haveibeenpwned.com
- Dehashed: https://www.dehashed.com
- Scylla.so: https://scylla.so - Intelligence X (search pastes): https://intelx.io

Geospatial Intelligence (GeoINT) Tools.

Geospatial tools help pinpoint locations, terrain, and environmental data via satellite imagery or image metadata.

Useful Tools:

- Google Earth Pro: 🔗 https://www.google.com/earth/versions/#earth-pro
- Sentinel Hub: 🔗 https://www.sentinel-hub.com
- Mapillary (street imagery): 🔗 https://www.mapillary.com
- Terraserver (satellite imagery): 🔗 https://www.terraserver.com

Automated OSINT Aggregation Platforms.

These platforms automate data collection from multiple sources and visualise relationships between entities.

Useful Tools:

- SpiderFoot: 🔗 https://www.spiderfoot.net
- Maltego: 🔗 https://www.maltego.com
- Recon-ng: 🔗 https://github.com/lanmaster53/recon-ng
- SOCMINT.io: 🔗 https://socmint.io

What is Artificial intelligence (AI).

AI (Artificial Intelligence)

Is the science and engineering of creating machines or software to perform tasks that typically require human intelligence. These tasks include:

Common AI Capabilities:

1. Understanding language – speech recognition, text generation, translation
2. Seeing and interpreting images – facial recognition, object detection
3. Learning from data – spotting patterns, making predictions
4. Making decisions – from game-playing to self-driving cars
5. Interacting with humans – chatbots, virtual assistants like Siri or ChatGPT

Types of AI:

1. Narrow AI (Weak AI) – AI that's trained for a specific task (e.g. Netflix recommendations, Google Maps)
2. General AI (AGI) – A theoretical AI that can do anything a human can (we don't have this yet)
3. Superintelligent AI – A future concept where AI exceeds human intelligence (still speculative)

How It Works:

Most modern AI relies on machine learning, where a system learns patterns from massive datasets rather than being explicitly programmed. For example:

• A machine learns to recognise cats by looking at thousands of photos.

• It adjusts itself to improve accuracy over time – this is training.

More advanced systems use deep learning, mimicking how the human brain works using layers of artificial "neurons."

Everyday Examples:

• Voice assistants like Alexa or Siri

• Spam filters in your email

• Self-driving features in cars

• Chatbots like this one (ChatGPT)

The use of AI in online investigations:

1. Research Assistant

• Tool and resource discovery: Ask ChatGPT for lists of up-to-date OSINT tools, browser extensions, or niche search engines.

• Explain how to use tools: Get walkthroughs on tools like Maltego, SpiderFoot, or Sherlock.

• Keyword and Boolean search builder: Generate custom search strings for Google Dorking or social media queries.

2. Persona Development

• Create investigative identities: Generate realistic backstories, usernames, and online behaviour traits for sock puppet accounts (used for passive research).

• Language and tone guidance: This helps craft posts or messages that align with the persona's background or target region.

3. Social Media Investigations

• Username investigation: Suggest platforms to search across (like using WhatsMyName, Namecheckr).

• Profile analysis tips: Learn what to look for in photos, bios, comments, and interactions.

• Link analysis: Assist in visually mapping relationships between accounts, posts, or hashtags (when paired with visual tools).

4. Image and Video OSINT

• Reverse image search techniques: We will guide you using tools like Yandex, TinEye, Google Lens, or EXIF viewers.

• Geolocation tips: Explain how to match visual clues (e.g., architecture, landmarks) with map data.

• Metadata investigation: Walkthroughs on extracting and analysing image/video metadata using tools like ExifTool.

5. Document & File Analysis

• Metadata extraction: Help interpret output from tools like FOCA or PDFinfo.

• QR code decoding: Explain how to extract embedded data and potential security implications.

• Text analysis: Summarise large files or documents, extract names, dates, entities, and generate timelines.

6. Email and Domain OSINT

• Email verification: Step-by-step use tools like Hunter.io, EmailRep, or MailTester.

• Domain & IP lookups: Guide you through Whois, DNSDumpster, Shodan, or Riskiq queries.

• Infrastructure mapping: Help you trace related domains or subdomains via passive DNS and historical data tools.

7. Dark Web and Threat Intel

• Access tips: Explain how to access the Dark Web safely using Tor and Tails OS.

• Onion link search: Help generate Boolean strings to search Onion sites (legally).

• Threat actor profiling: Assist in creating structured profiles from forum posts, aliases, or known patterns.

8. Report Writing and Case File Compilation

• Generate investigation reports: Format findings into structured reports with timelines, references, and summaries.

• Redact sensitive info: Help identify and obscure sensitive data in reports.

• Create templates: Offer templates for intelligence logs, evidence collection, and interview summaries.

9. Limitations

- Cannot access real-time or private data
- Does not replace specialised tools
- Should not be used to break terms of service or conduct surveillance on private individuals
- Data Volume: Analysts are overwhelmed—AI helps triage, but risks false positives.
- Fake Content: AI is also used to generate deepfakes, spam, and propaganda.
- Ethical Boundaries: Privacy, legality of scraping, and cross-border data laws are hotly debated.

Use of Artificial intelligence (AI) for OSINT Investigations.

Utilising ChatGPT for OSINT Investigations

Aida Kokanovic's four-part series demonstrates how generative AI can assist in OSINT tasks such as identifying website owners, analysing web technologies, and uncovering inter-website connections. ChatGPT is highlighted as a valuable tool for directing investigations, providing resources, and supporting analysis. https://shorturl.at/MzuJs

ChatGPT for Digital Forensic Investigation: The Good, the Bad, and the Unknown

A 2023 study assesses ChatGPT's capabilities in digital forensics, including artefact understanding, evidence searching, and anomaly detection. The research concludes that while ChatGPT can be a valuable supporting tool for knowledgeable users, it also poses risks due to potential inaccuracies and the need to validate its outputs carefully. https://shorturl.at/qeWij

The Slow Collapse of Critical Thinking in OSINT Due to AI

An article by a Dutch OSINT Guy warns about the gradual decline in critical thinking among analysts who increasingly depend on AI tools like ChatGPT. He emphasises the importance of maintaining analytical rigour and not allowing AI to replace human judgment in investigations. Nico Dekens🔗https://shorturl.at/Y8IU6

ChatGPT Search Tool Vulnerable to Manipulation and Deception

A Guardian investigation reveals that ChatGPT's search tool can be manipulated through hidden content on webpages, leading to biased or inaccurate responses. This vulnerability highlights the need for users to critically evaluate AI-generated information and be aware of potential manipulation tactics.

- OSINT Workflow with ChatGPT: Tips, Risks, and Benefits
- OSINT Combine discusses how ChatGPT can be incorporated into OSINT workflows to enhance efficiency. The article provides tips for practical prompt engineering, outlines potential risks, and explores the benefits of integrating ChatGPT into investigative processes.

ChatGPT for OSINT Analysts: Your AI-Powered Assistant for Organising Collected Intelligence

Ervin Zubic's publication highlights how ChatGPT can assist OSINT analysts in automating the organisation, tagging, and retrieving intelligence data.🔗 https://shorturl.at/vKW7P

ChatGPT for OSINT: Tips, Precautions, and Ethical Considerations
An article by Authentic8 discusses the integration of ChatGPT into OSINT workflows, emphasising the importance of continuous education and ethical considerations. It highlights the potential of generative AI to enhance investigative research while cautioning against overreliance and underscoring the need for human oversight.
🔗 https://www.authentic8.com/blog/chatgpt-for-osint

The best AI tools for OSINT depend on your goals.

1. ChatGPT (with plugins or custom GPTS) 🔗 https://shorturl.at/2aJdU

Best All-Around AI Assistant for OSINT ChatGPT (with plugins or custom GPTS)
• Great for research assistance, report writing, summarising intelligence, and generating search queries.
• Use it for: Boolean string creation, persona generation, metadata explanation, and scripting.
• Can integrate with Bing search, file readers, and code interpreters, or be trained with OSINT data.

2. AI for Image & Video OSINT

Hive AI / Sighthound 🔗 https://thehive.ai
• Great for facial recognition, object detection, and surveillance footage analysis.
• Used by: Law enforcement and commercial analysts for real-time and post-event video analysis.

Google Vision AI / Amazon Rekognition 🔗 https://shorturl.at/Ms7hi
• Great for: Image classification, OCR (text in images), label detection, and facial comparison.
• Used in: Reverse image verification, geolocation hints, image-based threat assessment.

3. AI Tools for Social Media OSINT

Maltego (with NLP add-ons) 🔗 https://www.maltego.com/transform-hub/tisane-labs
• Great for: Mapping digital footprints and social networks.
• AI integrations: NLP transformers or GPT APIS summarise relationships or infer connections.

Octoparse + GPT or ParseHub 🔗 https://research.aimultiple.com/octoparse-vs-parsehub
• Great for: Scraping social data, then summarising or analysing it using AI.

Silo for Research + Authentic8 AI
• Great for: Secure browsing + integrated AI assistant that supports OSINT workflows.
• Source: 🔗 https://www.authentic8.com

4. AI for Text & Metadata Analysis

Aleph by OCCRP
• Great for: Searching leaked or public records using AI-powered entity recognition.
• Open-source and searchable: 🔗 https://data.occrp.org

Hunchly + GPT 🔗 https://hunch.ly
• Great for: Web capture + AI summarisation.
• Used by: Investigative journalists and OSINT pros.

5. Dark Web & Threat Intelligence AI

DarkOwl Vision AI 🔗 https://www.darkowl.com/products/vision-app/
• Great for: Monitoring and extracting intel from darknet forums and marketplaces.
• Offers: AI-tagged entity extraction, risk scoring, and alerting.

Recorded Future 🔗 https://www.recordedfuture.com
• Great for: Threat intelligence using AI to monitor deep/dark web, forums, and more.
• Has a strong NLP backbone for contextual intelligence and predictive alerts.

Caveats

• AI tools require human validation, especially in legal or ethical contexts.
• Some require licenses or enterprise access (e.g., Palantir, Recorded Future).
• OSINT investigations should always follow legal and ethical standards.

UK AI Legal & Regulatory Framework (April 2025).

No Single AI Act:
The UK government does not have a single piece of legislation related to AI. Instead, it has opted for a flexible, pro-innovation framework that utilises existing laws to regulate AI development and deployment. This differs from the EU's AI Act.

Key Bodies & Guidance:

1. Information Commissioner's Office (ICO) – Data Protection
The ICO regulates AI under the UK GDPR and the Data Protection Act 2018. It focuses on:
- Automated decision-making
- Fair processing and transparency
- Lawful basis for AI processing. Key publications include the AI and Data Protection Risk Toolkit and the AI Auditing Framework.

2. Office for Artificial Intelligence – Policy Development
Part of the Department for Science, Innovation and Technology. Oversees the UK National AI Strategy to promote responsible AI innovation.

3. Digital Regulation Cooperation Forum (DRCF)
A collaboration between the ICO, Ofcom, Competition and Markets Authority (CMA), and Financial Conduct Authority (FCA). Publishes joint guidance on algorithmic and AI regulation.

4. Equality and Human Rights Commission (EHRC)
Ensures that AI applications comply with the Equality Act 2010, especially in preventing discrimination in automated decisions.

5. Sector-Specific Oversight Examples:
Healthcare AI Regulated by:
- MHRA (Medical devices)
- NHSX
- NICE (National Institute for Health and Care Excellence).

Financial AI Regulated by the FCA under:
- Senior Managers Regime
- Consumer Duty
- Anti-discrimination and fairness rules.

Police Use of AI/Facial Recognition Governed by:
- Human Rights Act 1998
- Surveillance Camera Code of Practice
- Relevant case law on proportionality and privacy.

6. Current Developments As of 2024–2025, the UK is exploring:
- Statutory guidance or binding rules for high-risk AI
- AI assurance and certification frameworks
- Strengthening the AI Safety Institute, launched in 2023.

Bibliography.

ACPO (2012) *Good Practice Guide for Digital Evidence*. [online] Available at: https://www.nationalcrimeagency.gov.uk

Bazzell, M. (2023) *Open Source Intelligence Techniques*. [online] Available at: https://inteltechniques.com

College of Policing (2021) *Digital Policing – Open Source Investigation*. [online] Available at: https://www.college.police.uk

College of Policing (2023) *Internet Investigation Training Resources*. [online] Available at: https://www.college.police.uk

Google (n.d.) *Google Advanced Search*. [online] Available at: https://www.google.com/advanced_search

Google (n.d.) *Google Hacking Database (GHDB)*. [online] Available at: https://www.exploit-db.com/google-hacking-database

ICO (n.d.) *UK GDPR guidance and resources*. [online] Available at: https://ico.org.uk/for-organisations/uk-gdpr-guidance-and-resources

IntelligenceTechniques (2023) *OSINT Techniques and Tools*. [online] Available at:
https://inteltechniques.com

Legislation.gov.uk (2016) *Investigatory Powers Act 2016*. [online] Available at:
https://www.legislation.gov.uk/ukpga/2016/25/contents

National Crime Agency (2020) *Cybercrime and Digital Investigation Manual*. [online] Available at:
https://nationalcrimeagency.gov.uk

NPCC (2021) *OSINT Guidance for Law Enforcement*. [online] Available at:
https://www.npcc.police.uk

Pariser, E. (2011) *The Filter Bubble: What the Internet is Hiding from You*. TED Talk. [online] Available at:
https://www.ted.com/talks/eli_pariser_beware_online_filter_bubbles

Pendergast, T. and Faltesek, D. (2018) *Digital Media Ethics*. London: Sage Publications.

Ratcliffe, J. (2009) *Intelligence-Led Policing*. Cullompton: Willan Publishing.

Rid, T. and Hecker, M. (2009) *War 2.0: Irregular Warfare in the Information Age*. London: Praeger Security International.

R v. McKeown [1997] 1 WLR 295

UK Government (n.d.) *Companies House*. [online] Available at: https://www.gov.uk/government/organisations/companies-house

Wayback Machine (n.d.) *Internet Archive*. [online] Available at: https://web.archive.org

Yandex (n.d.) *Search Engine*. [online] Available at: https://yandex.com

Zxing.org (n.d.) *QR Code Decoder*. [online] Available at: https://zxing.org/w/decode.jspx

Other Resources.

National Police Chiefs' Council (NPCC) (2021) Guidance on Open Source Investigation/Research. Available at: https://www.npcc.police.uk/SysSiteAssets/media/downloads/publications/disclosure-logs/workforce-coordination-committee/2023/061-2023-07-published-npcc-guidance-osint---reserach.pdf

Google (n.d.) Google Advanced Search. Available at: https://www.google.com/advanced_search

Google (n.d.) Google Scholar. Available at: https://scholar.google.com

LinkedIn (n.d.) LinkedIn Professional Networking Site. Available at: https://www.linkedin.com

Indeed (n.d.) Indeed Job Search Platform. Available at: https://www.indeed.co.uk

IntelTechniques (2023) Open Source Intelligence Techniques. Available at: https://inteltechniques.com

Facebook (n.d.) Facebook Social Networking Service. Available at: https://www.facebook.com

Twitter (X) (n.d.) Twitter (Now X) Social Platform. Available at: https://x.com

Internet Archive (n.d.) Wayback Machine. Available at: https://web.archive.org

Tineye (n.d.) TinEye Reverse Image Search. Available at: https://tineye.com

Yandex (n.d.) Yandex Images. Available at: https://yandex.com/images/search?from=tabbar

MXToolbox (n.d.) Email Header Analyser Tool. Available at: https://mxtoolbox.com/EmailHeaders.aspx

Glassdoor (n.d.) Glassdoor Job Reviews and Listings. Available at:
https://www.glassdoor.co.uk

Social Searcher (n.d.) Social Searcher Tool. Available at:
https://www.social-searcher.com

OpenCorporates (n.d.) The Open Database of Companies. Available at:
https://opencorporates.com

Ahmia (n.d.) Ahmia – Deep Web Search Engine. Available at:
https://ahmia.fi

Diffchecker (n.d.) Image Compare Tool. Available at:
https://www.diffchecker.com/image-compare

Let's Enhance (n.d.) AI Photo Enhancer. Available at:
https://letsenhance.io/signup

Invid (n.d.) Invid Verification Plugin. Available at:
https://www.invid-project.eu/tools-and-services/invid-verification-plugin

WebMii (n.d.) WebMii People Search. Available at:
https://webmii.com

Microsoft (2019). The Perils of Using Internet Explorer as Your Default Browser.
Available at:
https://rb.gy/hg6net

Mozilla (n.d.) Firefox Browser - Secure and Fast. Available at: https://www.mozilla.org/en-GB/firefox/new

Brave (n.d.) Brave Browser - Secure, Fast & Private. Available at: https://brave.com

Tor Project (n.d.). Tor Project. Available at: https://www.torproject.org

CCleaner (n.d.). CCleaner. Available at: https://www.ccleaner.com/ccleaner/download

Hunchly (n.d.) Hunchly Web Capture Tool. Available at: https://www.hunch.ly

Protonvpn (n.d.) Protonvpn Legality Blog. Available at: https://protonvpn.com/blog/are-vpns-illegal

ICANN (n.d.) Internationalised Domain Names (IDNS). Available at: https://www.icann.org/resources/pages/idn-2012-02-25-en

W3Schools (n.d.) HTML Basics. Available at: https://www.w3schools.com/html/html_basic.asp

ExifTool (n.d.). ExifTool by Phil Harvey. Available at: https://exiftool.org

IONOS (n.d.) Removing EXIF Data. Available at: https://www.ionos.co.uk/digitalguide/websites/web-design/removing-exif-data

Let's Enhance (n.d.) AI-Powered Image Enhancement. Available at: https://letsenhance.io/signup

Pic2Map (n.d.) EXIF Location Viewer. Available at: https://www.pic2map.com

Stolen Camera Finder (n.d.).Track Stolen Camera Equipment. Available at: https://www.stolencamerafinder.com

GeoSetter (n.d.) GeoSetter Software.Available at: https://geosetter.de/en/download-en

TED (n.d.) Eli Pariser – Beware Online Filter Bubbles. Available at: https://www.ted.com/talks/eli_pariser_beware_online_filter_bubbles

Search Engine Colossus (n.d.) Regional Search Engine Directory. Available at: https://www.searchenginecolossus.com

Matt W. (n.d.) YouTube GeoFind. Available at: https://mattw.io/youtube-geofind/location

ProtonMail (n.d.) Encrypted Email by Proton. Available at: https://proton.me/mail

Tutanota (n.d.) Secure Email Service. Available at:
https://tuta.com

Guerrilla Mail (n.d.) Disposable Email Address. Available at:
https://www.guerrillamail.com

Terms of Use for this eBook.

Copyright Infringement Policy.

We take intellectual property rights seriously. If you believe that content in our book infringes your copyright, please notify us at enquiries@opsimathy.co.uk with the following information:

- Your name and contact information
- A description of the copyrighted work
- The specific location (URL) of the infringing material
- A statement that you own the copyright or are authorised to act on behalf of the owner
- A statement that the information you provide is accurate to the best of your knowledge
- Your electronic or physical signature

Upon receiving a valid infringement notice, we will investigate and remove any content found to be in breach of copyright law.

www.ingramcontent.com/pod-product-compliance
Lightning Source LLC
La Vergne TN
LVHW090414210926
848480LV00002B/568

* 9 7 8 1 9 1 9 2 8 9 6 0 1 *